Hawk

An Inspiring Story of Success at the Game of Life and Baseball

Andre Dawson
with Tom Bird

ZondervanPublishingHouse

Grand Rapids, Michigan

A Division of HarperCollinsPublishers

Hawk: An Inspiring Story of Success at the Game of Life and Baseball
Copyright © 1994 by Andre Dawson and Tom Bird

Requests for information should be addressed to:
Zondervan Publishing House
Grand Rapids, Michigan 49530

Library of Congress Cataloging-in-Publication Data

Dawson, Andre
    Hawk / Andre Dawson with Tom Bird
      p.   cm.
    ISBN 0-310-49070-7
    1. Dawson, Andre. 2. Baseball players—United States—Biography. I. Bird, Tom,
1956–. II. Title.
    GV 865.D39A3 1994
    796.357'092—dc20
    [B]   94-29651
                                                  CIP

Edited by Verlyn D. Verbrugge
Cover design by John Lucas
Cover photos: Bill Smith, Damian Strohmeyer, Ronald C. Modra, John Garrett, Focus on Sports
Interior design by Sue Koppenol

Printed in the United States of America

94 95 96 97 98 99 /❖DH/ 10 9 8 7 6 5 4 3 2 1

This edition is printed on acid-free paper and meets the American National Standards Institute Z39.48 standard.

To my mother, Mattie Taylor,
my grandmother, Eunice Taylor,
and of course to my loving wife Vanessa.
ANDRE DAWSON

To my mother Irene Bird, and as always,
to my loving, supportive, and patient wife Barbara.
TOM BIRD

CONTENTS

FOREWORD

Andre Dawson is a man of many attributes. He is an excellent father, a supportive and caring husband, a compassionate son, a considerate brother, a faithful friend, and the hardest working, most determined ball player I have ever known.

Besides the attributes listed above, he also brings an infectious fire with him to everything he does. In every sense of the word, Andre Dawson is a champion.

All who touch his life, just by his example, better who they are. While with the Expos, Andre's presence saved Tim Raines's career and even his life from becoming a disaster. In recognition of Andre's influence, Raines named his first son after the future Hall of Famer. Andre was there for Shawon Dunston of the Cubs during the young shortstop's time of need as well. Andre's words also lifted newly acquired Hubie Brooks to a new level of play in Montreal. Andre's presence makes champions out of three to five players on each club he has played on and turns every person he is associated with into a winner.

If you gave Andre an IQ test, I can assure you that he'd grade out as a genius, a truly brilliant man. He inspires others by who he is and the example he sets. That's what blessedly smart people like Andre do.

You can feel the concentration and focus coming off him. Not many athletes have that. He stays on the positive plane of life, rising above the negative elements of life and using them to inspire himself to even greater heights. That's where the great humility that he possesses, as with all champions, comes from.

There is no one else like Andre Dawson. He is a living example of what a human being should be and can be. Amazingly, the influence he had while he was a Cub is still strongly felt years after he has moved on. In fact, I feel that what he left behind will never leave us. He touched us all—the players, the fans, everyone.

That same spirit, that same fire that is in Andre Dawson is embedded in this book. I am sure you will be a more appreciative, productive, and, most of all, joyful and faithful person as a result of reading this truly remarkable man's life story.

ERNIE BANKS
CHICAGO CUB HALL OF FAMER

ACKNOWLEDGMENTS

This book could have never been completed were it not for the unselfish assistance of so many of our friends, associates, and family members.

First of all, we would like to thank Mark Childers of Pro Promotions in Skokie, Illinois, for bringing the two of us together and for guiding us every step of the way.

Appreciation also needs to be extended to Mattie Taylor, Curtis Taylor, John Taylor, Warren Cromartie, Tim Raines, Costa Kittles, Billy Connors, Dick Moss, Dick Bresciani and his staff with the Boston Red Sox, Toni Larocca of the Montreal Expo Media Relations Department, all the members of the Chicago Cub Media Relations team, Barry Rozner, Joe Goddard, Dave Van Dyke, and Ned Colletti for their time, insight, and direction.

Thanks also belongs to Scott Bolinder of Zondervan, our publisher, for his always enthusiastic approach, and to John Sloan and Verlyn Verbrugge, our editors, for being so efficient, honest, creative, supportive, and giving.

Thanks also to Denis Brodeur of the Montreal Expos, Steve Green (team photographer of the Chicago Cubs), Publicity Department of the Boston Red Sox, personal photographer Dennis Brearly, and Alzheimer's Disease Research organization for supplying the pictures for the photo insert section.

We thank our families for sparing us the time and patience to make our tight deadline.

Thank you, most of all, Lord Jesus, for making this dream of ours a reality.

ANDRE DAWSON & TOM BIRD

CHRONOLOGY
OF ANDRE DAWSON

1954   Born July 10, 1954

1960   Baptized in his neighborhood church

1963   Plays his first Little League game

1971   Severely injures knee playing high school football

1972   Graduates from Southwest Miami Senior High;
         goes to Florida A & M and makes the baseball team

1975   Drafted by Montreal Expos; goes to Lethbridge, Alberta,
         minor league team

1976   Called up by Expos in September and gets first major
         league hit

1977   Named National League Rookie of the Year

1978   Marries wife Vanessa

1980   Wins first Golden Glove Award as a center fielder

1981   Starts first All-Star game; leads Expos to within one game
         of World Series

1983   Voted by peers as the Best Player in the Game

1984   Wins first Golden Glove Award as a right fielder

1986   Refuses the Expos' collusion-based offer

1987   Grandmother dies; signs with the Chicago Cubs for half
         of what Expos were offering; becomes National League
         Most Valuable Player

1989   Hits 300th career home run and logs 2000th hit;
         son Darius is born

1990   Daughter Amber is born

1992   Signs as a free agent with the Boston Red Sox

1993   Hits his 400th career home run

1994   Recurring knee problems convince him to retire

PART ONE

Where It All Began

CHAPTER ONE

The Gift of a Lifetime

A s an opposing player, what affects you the most in Wrigley Field is the fans' closeness to the field. Built exclusively for baseball, there are no bad seats in that stadium. The Cub fans, the most knowledgeable and vocal in baseball, are right on top of you—especially in right field, where I play.

I will never forget a voice that yelled out to me from the bleachers during my final trip to Chicago as a member of the Montreal Expos in 1986. Though I was the career leader in about every offensive career category for Montreal, it was becoming apparent to me that my time as an Expo was unfortunately coming to an end. The club no longer wanted me. The contract offer that the Expos had made, a substantial cut in pay, was at best insulting. Nothing either my agent or I said to them made any difference. I had desperately wanted to retire as an Expo, and the fact that I might not be able to do so was terribly frustrating for me.

By the time I had gotten to Wrigley for that final series in 1986, I had learned to take all the anger and frustration that I had previously internalized and to turn it loose on the baseball. I had my best games of the season during that series against the Cubs. It was during the final game of that series that the voice came to me from out of the bleachers.

"Forget those Canadians," the well-informed fan called down, knowing that I would reluctantly be testing the free agent market only a few months later. "Come on and play for the Cubbies. We'd love to have you."

Though I didn't acknowledge that voice with a tip of the cap or even a nod, what that one fan said affected me greatly. When negotiations finally broke down between me and the Expos, I had decided that Chicago was where I wanted to play, and I was willing to take a massive cut in pay just to play in the loving confines and soft grass of Wrigley Field.

Initially, the Cubs' management reacted pretty much as we had expected. They couldn't believe what I was doing, but that didn't keep them from biting on our offer. Within twenty-four hours of making the pitch to Chicago for which I will forever be remembered, I was a Cub.

Though I had not deliberately planned it that way, that action did more to solidify respect for me from the Chicago Cubs fans than anything else I could have done. I was a favorite of them long before I got my first standing ovation during my home opener as a Cub.

From that point on a magnificent love affair developed between the Cub faithful and myself. No player ever loved the fans of any city as much as I loved the Chicago fans, and I couldn't imagine any big leaguer ever being loved more than I was. It was a dream come true, an affection that seemed to feed both parties. They'd get on their feet and give me a standing ovation whenever I'd stride to the plate in a crucial situation, almost as if they expected me to deliver—and like magic, I always would.

My teammates just shook their heads and smiled each time it happened. They too couldn't believe what they were witnessing. At first all the attention embarrassed me. I'm basically an emotional, though shy and introverted person, and I didn't know how to react. Eventually, however, I began to loosen up and enjoy it, letting it feed my aching soul.

With the Cubbie faithful fully and vocally behind me, I was having a career year in 1987! Going into our final home game of the season, I was leading the league in home runs with 46, RBIs with 137, and game-winning hits with 16.

"MVP! MVP! MVP!" the packed house cheered, rising to their feet to greet me as I walked from our dugout to the on-deck circle for my final at-bat of the season at Wrigley.

It was one of those autumn days that is only possible at Wrigley. The ever-present wind was soft and steady. The cornucopia of brightly colored leaves adorning the outfield walls swayed gently. It was a high sky that day, without a cloud in sight and warm enough that many fans had dressed in white. Some of the bleacher faithful had even rid themselves of their shirts.

With every move I made the cheering got louder, "MVP! MVP! MVP!"

I could hear them, but I couldn't hear them. So blessed am I with the ability to concentrate that I can drown out any and all potential distractions. I could feel the muscles in my face begin to tighten and my eyes begin to sharpen as the familiar stare I had become so notorious for began to appear.

Mine is not a loud type of affection. I don't go screaming to the world how I feel. That's not me. Mine is a love illustrated through action. The fans wanted a home run, and I wanted to give it to them. All that was standing in the way was Cardinals pitcher Bill Dawley.

As I peered out at the imposing right-hander from that on-deck circle, I recalled how he had shut me down cold in our initial confrontations. I hated that. So I studied him to analyze why he had been able to do what so many other great pitchers had failed at. It was then that a conversation I had had a few years back with Hall of Famer Duke Snider, an announcer with the Expos, came to mind.

"Hawk, Rock, wait up." I recognized the voice immediately, realizing it was Duke trotting down the pavement toward me and my teammate and close friend, Tim Raines. We were waiting for the subway to take us to the team bus that was waiting for us at Olympic Stadium. From there, we would be driven to the airport to catch our flight to Houston, where we would be playing the Astros later that evening.

Duke is not one to mince words. He cut right to the chase. "They're jamming you inside, Hawk," he said, slightly out of breath.

I was hitting around .300 at the time, but I had not been driving the ball as I should have for quite some time. Obviously, Duke had noticed.

"They do that to tall guys like you who like to get their arms extended," he continued. I just listened. "You're fouling off pitches that you should be hitting out of the ball park."

I could feel the stare begin to form on my face as I listened intensely to what Duke, who had hit 407 big league homers, had to say. "I was able to take a ball as much as six inches off the plate, drive it, and keep it in fair territory."

He assumed a batting stance.

"You've got to tuck your fanny under like this," he said, demonstrating, "and bring your hands in against your body. Do you understand.?"

I just nodded.

That night in the Astrodome, a hitters' graveyard where the lights are dim and the air is still, I took the Astros deep for a pair of homers and a double. Two pitches on the fists, one mistake, resulted in ten total bases and four RBIs, making me the first visiting player to the Astrodome that season to hit two homers in one game.

What Duke had shared with me that day in Montreal suddenly came to mind, offering me a solution on how to hit Dawley. As I rose from the batting circle and strode toward home plate, the cheers got louder, rising to an almost deafening level, "MVP! MVP! MVP! MVP!"

I took the first two pitches, tempting offers by Dawley, but out of the strike zone. The crowd was going berserk. They were all on their

feet, cheering wildly. The more fanatical ones in the right field bleachers were even fully extending their arms and bowing to me, "salaaming" me, as it had been tabbed earlier in the season. I looked away
immediately so as not to break my concentration on the task at hand.
Dawley's next pitch was ball three.

In an effort to set him up, I took Dawley's fourth offering, a
blazing fast ball slicing directly across the outer half of the plate. Strike
one. I had him just where I wanted him. I would be ready.

Though I knew it would be ludicrous to swing for the fences—
no good hitter ever deliberately does that—I dug my back foot into
the soft turf of the batter's box, securing a firm hold that would enable
me to hit the ball hard.

By then, the fans could smell the answer to their prayers. Our
souls worked in unison. Sure enough, Dawley threw it, I hit it, they
loved it. I actually thought some of the fans, screaming so loudly from
the upper deck, might be in danger of falling out of their seats and over
the railing.

They reacted as if they had hit the home run themselves. And
in a way they had, for their love and faith had fed me that entire season. That home run, like all my other game-winning hits during that
year, was just my way of acknowledging how much their affection and
enthusiasm had meant to me.

As I touched first base and headed to second, the stare disap-
peared. The emotion of the moment had finally swept over me. I broke
into a full-fledged sweat and chills ran up and down my spine.

After the final out of the inning, the fans rose to their feet to
greet me as I ran out to my familiar spot in right field. The bleacher
bums were salaaming me.

Up to that time, the most I had ever done to the fans was
politely to tip my cap. However, that day, as I had told a teammate in
the dugout after I'd hit that 47th homer of the year, if they salaamed
me, I was going to go way outside of my character by salaaming them
back, which is exactly what I did.

The place went wild. Tears began to dampen my eyes and, out of embarrassment, I immediately turned back toward the infield and looked up to the sky. I knew at that moment, like I had known all season long, that she was there. Goose bumps began to appear as I whispered, "Thank you, Mamma, and thank you, Lord Jesus."

I could have retired right at that moment, for all that I had wanted to accomplish as a ballplayer and all that I had wanted to do to please her loving soul had been fulfilled.

With my grandmother's image appearing in my mind, I was with her as I usually was so early in my life. She was on her knees, looking directly at me. I was sitting in a chair, innocently listening to her speak.

"Andre," she said softly, "I have something very special that I want to show you, something that will change your life for the better. So listen up, all right, sweetie?"

I nodded.

"Andre, do you know who God is?" she asked.

I shook my head no.

"God is the maker of all things, the Father of us all."

I listened intently, the stare beginning to cross my face.

"Do you want to talk to God, son? Do you want to tell Him how much you love Him and how thankful you are for all that He has given you?"

I nodded.

"Do you know how to do that, Andre? Do you know how to pray?"

I shook my head.

"You take your hands like this," she said, gently positioning my hands to pray. "Then you close your eyes."

I did so.

"Open your heart and talk to the Lord, speak to Jesus," she said, pausing. "That's all that you have to do to pray."

I opened my eyes.

"But how do I know if he'll hear me?" I asked.

She chuckled. "Because God hears everything and answers every prayer. Do you want to try praying?"

I nodded.

"Even better, son, how would you like to pray together?" she asked with a grin.

I responded immediately. I loved doing just about anything with her.

"Okay, Andre, let's hold our hands like this, close our eyes and. . . ."

She was absolutely right. What she would teach me that day would change my life.

PART TWO

Born to Play Baseball

CHAPTER TWO

Roots

Reading the Bible and praying were how my ancestors dealt with the heartache, deprivation, and repression that life, especially that of the black man, carries with it. The Bible was the only book that the plantation owners, for whom my ancestors worked as slaves, would allow them to read. It was the only formal education available; but it was the best type they could get, and it was all they needed. So important to my family was reading the Bible that my great-grandfather, Edward Harrell, taught himself to read by reading it to his father, my great-great-grandfather, who had gone blind.

Ed Harrell was born in the middle of one of the country's most racist areas, a place called Hawkinsville, Georgia, just a little south of Macon. During his lifetime, lynching was still prevalent. Only two generations removed from his slave ancestors, he did his best, like his father, to farm a dusty, hilly, rocky scrap of land that the rich land-owners didn't want.

In between constant droughts, boll weevil attacks, and the Great Depression, my great-grandfather did his best to scrape out a living for his family, farming whatever he could, from sweet potatoes to corn. He even farmed a little cotton to sell off at the market if he could come up with the money for the seed. He also hunted anything—rabbits, squirrels, possum—to help feed his family.

That was the heritage that this small man with a big heart carried with him out of the family's homestead in Hawkinsville, relocating his young family in 1926 to the promised land of Miami, Florida. At the time Miami was not much more than deserted swamp land, surrounded by miles and miles of beach.

In our family, every person's life was seen as a ministry. My self-taught, charismatic great-grandfather soon became a deacon of the local Baptist church and the spiritual epicenter of the three-block-by-three-block middle class, black neighborhood into which I was eventually born. Known as a man who never turned anyone away and would gladly give you his last nickel, he and my great-grandmother were lovingly referred to by everyone in the community as "Grandpa and Grandma," or as "Uncle Ed and Aunt Alice."

As a wise man, my great-grandfather's ministry was built around offering sound advice on just about any subject, advice that would be easy to digest and follow. He could understand even the most complicated of novels or pieces of art and translate their meaning in the simplest, most easy-to-understand ways.

He had never taken a drink in his life. "If you're going to be a man, be a man," I often heard him counseling my uncles. "You don't have to prove anything to anybody by pouring booze inside of you."

He was also a real leader. Whether in church, at your job, with your family, or with your friends, he was always firmly counseling on the value of leading by example. "If you want somebody to do something," he always said, "show them how to do it by doing it yourself first."

When he talked, people always listened. Not only neighbors and the local pastor, but also the generous white man Mr. Slocum, for whom he worked as a sharecropper, sought his advice. So valued was my great-grandfather's friendship with Slocum that it is said that they looked at each other as brothers. In fact, people recalled how Slocum would openly let Ed Harrell drive his truck, something unheard of in those days of strict segregation.

My uncles, aunts, and mother had such great feeling for Ed Harrell that they wouldn't do anything wrong as children—not out of fear but out of respect for him.

What I remember most about my great-grandfather are the family prayer meetings he used to hold at dawn every Christmas and Easter. All my cousins, aunts, uncles, brothers, and sisters would meet at my great-grandparents' home promptly at sunrise, and he'd ask the entire family to kneel while he prayed. I'll never forget those days or the heartfelt and elegant way in which he came to the Lord before all of us, a living example I will never forget.

My great-grandparents both died in their early nineties. Neither had any specific diseases or ailments. No one even remembered them being sick a day in their lives. They both just drifted off, the way I believe that the Lord meant for death to be.

After their passing, their eldest child, Eunice Taylor, my grandmother, took over as the spiritual pillar of the community. Married before moving with my great-grandparents to Miami, she bore four children to my grandfather: my mother, Mattie, who was the oldest, and her three brothers, Curtis, John, and Theodore.

I was born when my mother was fifteen years old. She was a sophomore in high school at the time. My father, Floyd Dawson, a few years older than my mother, had met her at high school. But once I was born, he refused even to acknowledge my presence. When I was still young, he headed off to college and then went into the military. During his time in the U. S. Army, he saw plenty of action in Vietnam and was decorated several times. Eventually, he proudly retired as a major general and returned home with his family to nearby Coconut Grove, where he had grown up.

Because my father did little in terms of child support to offset the expense of raising me, my mother was basically left on her own. Thank God for my grandmother, who stepped in immediately with her ever-ready hand.

My grandmother was the closest person to God I have ever met. She never had anything but praise for everything and everyone. When most people would have found it easy to reject my mother and me in our situation, my grandmother, whom I just called "Mamma," saw only the beauty in life.

My mother was always either going to school or working well into the evening as a baker at Toby's Cafeteria in downtown Miami. Therefore, Mamma became my primary role model. To her I was not an illegitimate child. I was her first grandchild, her pride and joy, "li'l' Andre." She wheeled me around the neighborhood in my baby carriage or took me to church or to prayer meetings just so she could show me off to her friends. Though everyone in the neighborhood was well aware of the situation regarding my underage mother and estranged father, never once did anyone ever mutter a bad word. That's how great a respect they had for my grandmother and her family.

"If you want respect," she used to tell me, "you have to give it first. Live by the golden rule, Andre; do unto others the way you want them to do unto you." Like her father, she was always counseling, teaching, and sharing. That was her way, her ministry as well.

Never once did I ever see her frustrated, angry, or mad. Swearing was not part of her character. She was too filled with the power and love of the Lord to have any room left over for such unnecessary distractions. Not even when her husband, my grandfather, ran around on her did she lose control and turn to hatred. Even though they got divorced, she made sure that no one got hurt and no one got mad.

Even the family that she had worked for as a maid loved her. To them she was much more than just someone who came in, cleaned up, and cooked. She was their friend, a surrogate parent, and a fill-in grandparent to their children.

It was to this blessed woman that I woke up each day, the same one who usually laid me down to sleep each night, taught me how to tie my shoes, and helped me bake my first cake at the age of five, for my mother's birthday. As I grew older, she was the one to whom I came home from school and the one who disciplined me, taught me right from wrong, helped me with my homework and heartaches, and guided me through the responsibility I had for helping raise my seven younger brothers and sisters, whom my mother bore to my stepfather Clarence.

Mamma saw a blessing and an opportunity for joy and enlightenment in every moment and continually shared her insights with me. I was not only her favorite grandchild, whom she raised as if I were her own child; I was also her best student.

Many a night we sat around talking, after my long day had come to a close and I had concluded my final chores (washing and drying her nightly dishes for my next day's lunch money). She would teach me about life and about God over a piece of cake and a glass of milk. What she taught me programmed me for my entire lifetime.

Mamma was also the one that introduced me to the church. In our community the Mount Olive Baptist Church was more than just a place where you went to worship. It was where your birth was celebrated and your passing mourned. It was the home of meetings and socials. In fact, everything that happened in our neighborhood revolved around the church. No one ever had to force me to go there. Church was fun.

The closeness and trust that was bred in all of us and the love we had for each other through our constant association with the church made our neighborhood one big family. You could actually go away for a few days and leave your windows and doors open. If it rained, for example, one of your neighbors went in and shut your windows for you.

With us kids, it was as if we had a dozen parents. Everyone watched out for each other's kids and wasn't shy about disciplining someone else's child. So my friends and I always tried to be doubly good when we were growing up, because if you were bad, not only were you expected to endure the wrath of your own parents but some of the other adults in the neighborhood as well.

I don't remember the exact date or year (I think I was around six years old) when Mamma approached me about being baptized. In terms of importance, baptism was second to only marriages and funerals in our neighborhood. I still remember Mamma coming to me early one Sunday morning and saying, "Andre, would you like to be baptized?"

I wasn't quite sure what she was talking about. But with that sweet smile on her face there was no way that I would turn her down for anything. So whether I knew what she was talking about or not, whether I really wanted to be baptized or not, didn't really matter. I just nodded my head yes and did as she said.

First I had to officially join the church. In what seemed like no time at all, she had me dressed in my best Sunday clothes and was walking with me, with her hand gently wrapped around mine, toward the church. She paraded me up to the front pew with her as usual, and we sat down. After a good portion of the service had passed, she led me out into the aisle, gently kissed me on the cheek, whispered in my ear, "I'm very proud of you, son," and handed me over to the pastor.

The rest happened so fast that it seemed like a blur. The pastor mumbled a few words and pushed me under some cold, cold water. Still somewhat in shock by the whole series of events, I began looking for Mamma in the audience right after the pastor had loosened his grip. The look on her face had confirmed it all. My baptism had made her the proudest woman alive.

Shortly after that, my call to baseball began to manifest itself.

CHAPTER THREE

Help Along the Way

Most persons are born with a combination of purposes for their lives. But for each person, there is one main purpose. For some that may mean being a teacher, for others a parent, for still others a person of the law. For me, I was born to play baseball. My desire to swing a stick or a bat, whatever I could get my hands on when I was young, surfaced in my life long before I knew what baseball was. By the age of four I had broken off my first mop handle and scurried outside to hit some stones. At age six I sent my first rock flying through one of the neighbor's windows. By eight I had claimed my first (and only) windshield.

I was born in a nurturing environment—as it says in Matthew 13:8, "on good soil." My ancestors, grandmother, mother, uncles, and aunts had seen to that. Because of my supportive family, my love for and appreciation of the game of baseball was never once questioned. In fact, it was applauded by my mother's brothers—Curtis, John, and Theodore (whom we called Sugar Bo)—who were a combination surrogate fathers/big brothers to me. They became not only the fertilizer but the tenders of the baseball crop I produced.

From them, I learned to play the game and to love the Brooklyn (soon-to-become Los Angeles) Dodgers. Why they loved the Dodgers so much, I don't know. Was it because Jackie Robinson broke the color barrier with the club? Or maybe because the Dodgers were just a great team? Or perhaps they loved them so much because the Dodgers used to play a few exhibition games each spring at nearby Miami Stadium? I don't know. But what I do know is that I loved those Dodgers almost as much as I loved life itself.

I ate, slept, and dreamt Dodgers. I listened to every one of their games that I could. When I was old enough, I began making up mock box scores—the Dodgers against this team, the Dodgers against that team. Of course, the Dodgers never lost a game, and my favorite players, Jim Gilliam, Sweet Lou Johnson (I loved the way the Dodger public address announcers used to say his name, Sweet Louuuuuu), and Tommie Davis always got the big hits.

When the Dodgers played the Yankees in the 1963 World Series, and for every other fall classic that Los Angeles appeared in during my youth, I skipped school to stay home and watch the game on television.

Each of my three uncles brought something unique and different to the garden of my life. Curtis, the oldest, offered me wisdom and leadership. His calling was to be a teacher, eventually working his way up to vice principal in one of the local elementary schools. He watched over me in a paternal way. Even today Curtis still constantly checks with me or my wife, Vanessa, on how I'm doing or how I'm feeling. It's wonderful to know that I can turn to Curtis at any time for the guidance, wisdom, and honesty that a man needs throughout his life.

The middle boy, John, has been a combination big brother and younger father to me. In contrast to Curtis, who is outspoken, he is usually silent, preferring to remain in the background. Yet he is there at a moment's notice if I need him.

John has a heart of gold. Like Mamma, he doesn't have a negative bone in his body. Later in my career, when I wanted to find an efficient way to fund charities, John was the one who gave me the idea to start a foundation.

In his own quiet way, John was probably the finest athlete of the three. His forte was running. As a kid, he was always challenging his baby brother Bo, or anybody else he could find, to a race. Young Sugar Bo would race him from my great-grandparents' house back to their home, a distance of about a quarter of a mile. Being fair-minded, John always spotted his younger brother fifteen or twenty yards in front of him, which would make for one great race, especially the last fifty yards. According to John, he never once lost to his younger brother. Tales of some of the races were legendary around our neighborhood.

A bout with rheumatic fever cut short his athletic career. From that point forward, my grandmother forbade her precious son to participate in strenuous activities. I can only wonder how good John would have been in track, baseball, or any other sport he had chosen if he hadn't gotten the fever.

Bo, only nine years my senior, played the role of an older brother. He eventually became the most accomplished athlete of the three. In track, he was named to the All-Miami Black Track Team during his senior year in high school. Bo was so fast that he even once outran eventual Olympic gold medalist Bob Hayes.

On the baseball diamond, Bo, like all of the black athletes growing up in the Miami area, had to battle segregation. In fact, it was because of segregation that he didn't get to play his first organized baseball game until his senior year at high school. Yet, even with so little formal training, he made it as far as Charleston of the AAA International League, one step away from the Pittsburgh Pirates and the majors.

After Bo asked for his release from the Charlies, we worked out together and hung out daily. I used the time to pick his brains about the ins and outs of pro baseball, and he was more than happy to share what he had learned with me. His continual guidance helped me better understand the inner workings of the game and to prepare for what I felt I was destined to do.

While segregation had halted the potential sports careers of my uncles and others of their generation, Curtis was determined that I and the other boys in our neighborhood would not suffer the same fate. When the city refused any financial assistance for our youth sports, he decided to start a little league of his own. My uncle John was right in there along with his older brother, and I'm sure Bo would have been too if he hadn't been off playing minor league ball.

Skeptics thought that Curtis was crazy. But his bubbling disposition got the project rolling, and soon everyone was pitching in, raising money through fund raisers and soliciting donations. My mom chipped in with endless hours, personally blanching fifty pounds of peanuts to sell at the games. The enthusiasm of neighbors and parents was contagious, and in no time their efforts netted the bats, balls, bases, gloves, helmets, caps, and tee-shirts needed to launch our first season.

I will never forget that first season. The constant competition made me love the game all the more. And I also learned a lot, one of the main lessons being not to step outside my role as a player and to question authority.

Our team was fortunate enough to appear in the championship game. To me it was the biggest game of my life—as big as any one of the Dodgers four games against the Yanks in the 1963 series. In reality, I was a little too pumped, as I would later find out.

As usual, I arrived early for the game. Unfortunately, our coach was late, and I began to get nervous. Out of desperation I tried to tell my uncle Curtis, who was coaching our opponent for the game but was also trying to help us out by filling out our line-up card, who should bat where. My persistence caused my usually patient uncle to lose his cool and bench me for the game. I was crushed. In fact, I was so brokenhearted and confused that I had to have a heart-to-heart talk with Mamma after the game. She listened attentively before offering me her evaluation of the situation.

"Pudgy," she said to me, calling me by my most popular nickname, "your job as a player is to play, not coach. So by trying to coach when your only job was to play, you were being disrespectful. Your uncle had every reason to bench you."

The lesson I learned that day gave me a lot of insight about myself. It was the last time I ever let my natural competitive instinct get the better of me. Since then, I have never complained to either a coach or manager.

Despite my lack of proper judgment in the championship game, I performed well enough during the season to land myself a spot on the twelve- and thirteen-year-old all-star team. Though I mainly handled the club's score-keeping chores, I went along when we traveled to a distant part of Miami to play an all-white all-star team. That marked the first of several experiences, and possibly the most pleasant, that taught me a significant lesson on how the game should be played.

Though we whipped the all-white team soundly, they eventually brought in older kids to whip our younger kids. So Uncle Curtis good-naturedly countered by bringing in *our* older kids, who whipped them again. No one got mad; it was all in good fun. Both teams gladly shook hands and went home happy. That's how everyone should play the game of baseball!

The successes and joys I experienced playing in my uncle's baseball league further confirmed for me what I knew I had to do with my life, though I had trouble convincing other people of that. I remember once in junior high when my classmates and I were asked to answer a vocational interest questionnaire, to better help our counselors structure individual curricula over our remaining years in school. To the question what I wanted to be, I wrote down "a major league ball player."

When my counselor read over my responses, she smirked and said to me in an unbelieving tone, "Okay Andre, what do you *really* want to be?" She didn't believe me or believe in me—or maybe both. But I had been completely honest with her, and I fully believed that I would become what I felt God wanted me to be. Her response bothered me. So, as always, I sought out the reliable and loving counsel of Mamma.

In one of the most important discussions I would have with her, she introduced me to the presence of devils in my life.

CHAPTER FOUR

The Devils
Mamma Told Me About

If you have given your heart to God and accepted Jesus Christ as your Lord and Savior, there is no way you can be adversely affected from the inside. You have no room for corruption or wrongdoing, for you are filled to the brim with the Holy Spirit. However, no matter how faithful they are, Christians can be severely influenced by exterior forces. That's what my grandmother was trying to warn me about when she had her discussion with me about devils.

"Devils," she had told me, "are not little Lucifers. They're usually just lost or misguided souls who haven't accepted Christ as their Savior and thus haven't allowed the Holy Spirit to take over their lives.

"As a result, negative presences in the world often overpower them. In turn, you have to be on guard so that these negative presences don't influence you through them. If you're filled with the Holy Spirit, like you Andre, that's the only way that the negative forces of the world cannot get to you.

"Listen to yourself, son. Weigh alternatives and situations before making decisions. If you don't feel right about something, don't do it. Maybe you don't understand why you feel a certain way, but God is trying to warn you. If you're a Christian, that will happen to you a lot. That's one of the ways that he takes care of us and protects us from all the traps and temptations that await us in life."

In 1971, as a seventeen-year-old junior at Southwest High School in South Miami, I discovered exactly what she meant. I was one of only a few black students in the predominantly all-white school, though that is not what caused me trouble. Even when I was in South Miami Junior High I had listened to myself and stayed clear of the race riots following the assassination of Martin Luther King in 1968. But during the fall of 1971, I made an inappropriate decision not to listen to myself, a decision that has caused me incredible pain ever since.

As if it happened only yesterday, I remember the warning I should have heeded. Because all of my best buddies had gone out for the football team, I decided to try out as well. Already then I had a strong throwing arm, so most of my buddies thought that I should play quarterback. The coach convinced me to try my luck at free safety instead. He supposedly had too many other boys who wanted to play quarterback, with whom he had been working a long time, so that my chances of seeing much action were slim. So I reluctantly accepted his suggestion and shifted my bony little body over to the defensive side of the ball.

During one of our practices, one of our tight ends came across the field to block me. In an attempt to intercept a quick pass over the middle, I slipped on the muddy practice field and fell on my back. Just as I did, our tight end's spikes slipped through my face guard and ripped a large gash into my right cheek. It took eight stitches to close it back up; I still have the scar.

Right after that I quit the team. I felt that I had a baseball career to protect, and there was no way that I was going to allow it to be ruined by playing football. Eventually, however, I allowed one of the assistant coaches to talk me into coming back to the team, and I won back my starting position at free safety.

Our fourth game of the season was against North Miami. Two minutes remained in the first half when I, smelling an interception, dropped back into pass coverage. The interception never materialized, but something more dramatic unfortunately did.

A North Miami receiver blocked one of our corner backs into me, and his helmet struck my left knee. I went down immediately. Rolling back and forth on the field in pain, I knew that I was seriously hurt. When I tried to stand, I couldn't. My leg wobbled like Jello. The trainers insisted I had only strained a ligament in my knee, and they sent me home.

Later that night I started to get a burning sensation in my leg and found it impossible to sleep. The next morning my mother took me to the hospital. An orthopedic surgeon diagnosed me as suffering from torn cartilage and ligaments. I was admitted immediately and had surgery the following morning.

Though such an injury today is easily treated without any long-term damage, the surgeon at that time removed all of the medial cartilage from my left knee, common practice in 1971. Cartilage is the lining that allows the joints to glide over each other. Without it a knee becomes arthritic, and the constant rubbing keeps it chronically inflamed. In addition, the constant swelling creates bone chips. Regular clean-up and maintenance are the only alternatives; repair is no longer an option. I have had to live with that situation ever since that accident.

I was in the hospital for five days before being released with a thigh-high cast on my leg. I was so bitter and hostile about what had happened that I refused to go to school. There was no way that I was going to let myself hobble around with that cast, a constant reminder of my refusal to listen to the Lord. I asked my Mom to get me a tutor, which she did.

After the doctor removed my cast, he did not prescribe any rehab or physical therapy. My rehab came through running around on the baseball field and straining to do what had always come so easily to me. Even though my throwing and batting skills had not diminished, my condition did affect me. With a big brace strapped to my knee, none of the pro scouts, who had dogged me so diligently the year before, came out to see me play.

I didn't begin to recover any strength in my knee until near the conclusion of our season. By that time our coach had moved me from third base, where he said I was handcuffing the other infielders with my strength and fierce throws, out to left field. Fumbling around in the outfield as I tried to learn my new position didn't do much to attract interest from scouts either.

Yet my love for the game grew stronger every day. I felt deeply that there was still some way to fulfill what I believed was my destiny. I did exactly what my grandmother had taught me. With every bit of faith I could muster, I turned the entire situation over to the Lord and made a decision to leave the solution up to Him. I promised myself and God that I would believe in Him, follow the designs he had for me, and do whatever it took, in Jesus' name, to fulfill His calling for me. Almost immediately I experienced a new-found fire of commitment and desire to play baseball.

The following summer I heard about a tryout camp that the Kansas City Royals were hosting at the University of Miami. The Royals' scouts were going to be trying out kids for their newly established baseball academy, a sort of a cross between a college and a professional training center, with the emphasis on the latter. Like all of my buddies from the baseball team, I was excited simply to try out before a group of big league scouts.

As soon as I heard about the tryout I couldn't wait to share the news with somebody. That somebody, as you might expect by now, was my grandmother.

"You want to do what?" she asked emphatically.

"I want to go to the tryout," I replied sheepishly. I was caught somewhat off-guard by her reaction. I had thought that she would be excited for me. But after mentioning it to her, I realized how far her wisdom exceeded my understanding at that time.

"Pudgy, you know how important it is to get an education," she said softly. As a loving smile appeared across her face, she continued, "Just because they call it an academy doesn't mean that it's a college, a university, or any kind of school. Don't let them fool you. Don't let any potential devils take advantage of you or lead you away from where the Lord wants you to go."

In my heart and mind I knew she was right, but I decided to go to the tryout anyway. For that same voice I had felt telling me to quit football was now telling me to go. I really wasn't interested in being invited to attend the academy. I just wanted to see if I was good enough to make it. I wanted to confirm everything I felt the Lord had been leading me to do. So I strapped on my knee brace, picked up my glove, and headed out.

Going to that tryout constituted a big step for me. Up until then I had fed off of the faith that my mother, uncles, aunts, and particularly my grandmother had with the Lord. I had never stepped outside their shadows to meet and connect with God on my own.

On the way to the field, I kept pondering a bit of advice that my grandmother had once offered me, repeating it over and over again in my mind. "Pudgy," she had said, "pray and believe in yourself, and you will always be granted the ability to hear the Lord's reply."

To say that I was a little bit nervous that morning is an understatement. Of the three hundred or so players that showed up for the tryout, I was one of the youngest. Most of the players were college-age men. I was also one of only a few black players. That wasn't new to me, of course. I had become used to jumping over, running around, or charging through racial barriers.

Despite my age and knee brace, I hit every pitch thrown to me that morning. I could hear the Kansas City scouts standing around the batting cage talk about me as I took my swings. They were impressed, and I knew by the end of the day that I stood an excellent chance of being invited back the next day. Sure enough, I was one of three players asked to come back the following morning.

Outside of my burning desire to play baseball, I'm a very laid-back type of guy. Usually nothing rattles me. However, I must admit that I tossed and turned that entire night. I fully agreed with Mamma's view of the academy. And I also agreed with her that if God truly wanted me to play baseball, I wouldn't have to jump desperately at the first offer that might come to me. The Lord would surely lead me to a situation that was better suited for me.

Yes, I was frightened that the coaches might choose me. How would I tell them that I wouldn't be able to accept their offer to attend their baseball academy, a school that millions of kids my age would have sold their soul to be invited to? All night long I wrote down and rehearsed my turn-down speech. The next day, I showed up at the try-out. Thank God I didn't have to use that speech. My prayers had been answered. They didn't choose me. They said I was too slow. Whew!

But what was I to do now? Even though I was the first black player ever to make the Miami Times High School All-Star Baseball team, I wasn't offered a scholarship by any college or university. The Kansas City scouts suggested that I try out at Florida State University as a walk-on. That was the last I heard from them. But I had gotten what I had wanted and more. I had received the confirmation I had so sorely sought. Even more, I had established a stronger individual and personal connection with my Lord and Savior.

During my growing-up years, from the time I first broke off that mop handle through my first years of organized ball, baseball was going through massive changes that, unknown to me at the time, I would later be blessed to become an integral part of.

Through the 1950s, running a big league team constituted little more than a hobby for the owners of the teams. The players had no rights at all, not even the ability to choose what team they would play for.

By the early '60s, the players' bargaining position was strengthened by the expansion of the teams, causing a scarcity of talent throughout the majors. The owners countered in 1962 by making it mandatory for each club to subsidize at least five minor league teams.

In 1965, the owners ended the free enterprise system of scouting by establishing an annual draft of high school and collegiate players.

A year later, Dodger pitchers Don Drysdale and Sandy Koufax set a precedent in pro sports by using a lawyer in their contract negotiations. Later in 1966 the Major League Players Association hired a labor relations big wig, Marvin Miller, to take on the owners. Hoping to turn back the clock to the post-union struggles of the 1930s, Miller brought along with him energetic chief counsel Dick Moss, whom he had known from his days with the national Steelworkers Union.

In 1967, calling for better pension benefits, better working conditions, and minimum salaries for the big leaguers, Miller and Moss produced the first ever formal labor contract between the owners and players, commonly referred to as the basic agreement.

By 1969, with backing of Miller and Moss, St. Louis outfielder Curt Flood stepped forward to challenge baseball's reserve clause, a move for which he will forever be remembered. Claiming that trading him, catcher Tim McCarver, and pitchers Byron Browne and Joe Hoerner for first baseman Dick Allen, infielder Cookie Rojas, and pitcher Jerry Johnson, was "impersonal," Flood balked at his being sent from the pennant-contending Cards to the cellar-dwelling Phils and asked Major League Commissioner Bowie Kuhn to declare him a free agent. Kuhn denied his request.

In retaliation, Miller and Moss filed a lawsuit against major league baseball on January 16, 1970 on behalf of Flood, stating that baseball had violated the nation's antitrust laws. Even though Flood was making $90,000, an enormous salary at the time, he likened being traded without his consent to "being owned," as if he were like the slaves of a hundred years ago. The case eventually wound up with the

Supreme Court of the United States, where former Supreme Court Justice Arthur Goldberg, offering to handle the case for free, pleaded the case for the players.

Goldberg eventually won the case for the MLPA, and the Washington Senators acquired the rights to the estranged outfielder from Philadelphia for marginal players Greg Goosen, Jerry Terpho, and Gene Martin. Flood, after sitting out 1970, signed for $110,000. But after hitting only .200 for the Senators in their first twelve games, he retired from baseball.

Later in 1971, while plans for expansion were being drawn up, Miller and Moss negotiated a second addition to the basic agreement, winning the right for all players to use agents in salary negotiations.

The year 1972 was another stormy year for baseball. With Miller and Moss lighting the fuse, big leaguers, in an unprecedented action, staged a thirteen-day walk. The strategy worked. The owners, who had been forced to take the solidarity of the union seriously, reluctantly consented to sign a new agreement with the MLPA that allowed the players to seek binding arbitration in salary disputes. Though the far-reaching effects of this decision would take years to surface, when the results finally came around, they made front-page headlines in every newspaper across the country.

CHAPTER FIVE

A & M and Pop

Growing up black provides an individual with a unique set of bridges to cross and barriers to fight through. The key is not to allow oneself to fall prey to racist ways. Not absorbing another person's hatred of you by reacting to it is essential, for you are then leaving the disease right where it belongs, with the one who has it and who is the only one that can do anything about it.

That was a lesson I was to learn during my years at Florida A & M, an all-black school I chose to attend over the Kansas City scouts' recommendation of Florida State.

Why did I choose this school? First, since no universities or colleges were offering me any scholarships, I was free to try out as a walk-on at any school I wanted.

Second, since my uncles had all attended A & M, I decided to follow in their footsteps.

Third, A & M is a fine school. Located in Tallahassee, it opened its doors in 1887. During Bo's time there, it had experienced rapid growth. By the time I enrolled, A & M had already become a member of the Southern Intercollegiate Athletic Association of Colleges and had been accepted as a full partner in Florida's nine-university, public higher education system.

Fourth, it was no secret to folks in Miami that A & M had one of the finest sports programs in our area of the country. From an athletic department begun humbly in 1899 have come some of the greatest athletes this country has ever known.

For example, Althea Gibson, the first black to win a major tennis championship, was an A & M grad. The trailblazer for other black tennis stars such as Arthur Ashe, Althea won more than fifty major tennis tournaments, including the French Open in 1956 and Wimbledon and the U.S. Open in 1957 and 1958. She also appeared on the women's pro golf tour. Althea eventually received the prestigious Theodore Roosevelt Award, the highest honor bestowed by the National Collegiate Athletic Association, joining the company of such well-known celebrities as former U.S. Presidents Ronald Reagan and Gerald Ford and entertainer Bill Cosby.

Olympic Gold Medal sprinter and all-pro wide receiver for the Dallas Cowboys, Bob Hayes, was another A & M student, along with more than seventy other athletes who went on to play professional football. Rey Robinson, an Olympic sprinter who, like Hayes, set a world record in the 100-meter dash, also attended A & M.

The basketball program at A & M has created its share of stars, including Tommy Mitchell, who played with the Harlem Globetrotters, and Walt Bellamy and Leroy "Spike" Gibson, both of whom played in the National Basketball Association.

On the baseball front, A & M was also top shelf. For the last fifteen seasons, the Rattlers had been under the direction of Costa "Pop" Kittles, one of the closest men to the Lord I had ever had the privilege of meeting. A former baseball and football player himself, Pop was hired in 1958 to coach both sports. What he learned while working under legendary gridiron mentor Jake Gaithers enabled him to become an outstanding leader.

Like Gaithers, who had led A & M to six national titles, produced 36 All-Americans, and yielded 42 professional football players, Pop, who had once been offered a contract by the Negro Leagues Newark Eagles, saw coaching as his ministry. Through Jake, Pop refined "the sharing of his blessings with others," as he often put it. He taught his players about life through the game. What he shared with them stayed with them long after their playing days were over.

"No one ever left Pop's company without having been moved," I remembered Bo once telling me.

Because Pop had thought so highly of Bo, I felt only a slight nervousness about meeting him for the first time, when I tried out for the team. Kittles made a point of making me feel at home immediately. "We heard you may be coming out," he said with a wink. "Glad you're here, son."

Though Costa's friendly demeanor never changed, the intensity that I was used to working out on the diamond did. From the very first time that he ran us through his typical series of drills, I could see that baseball at A & M was going to be a lot different than the laid-back game of pitch-and-hit I had experienced at Southwest High. I welcomed the changes and adapted quickly.

After exhibiting my skills early in the tryout period, I was offered a partial scholarship. By the conclusion of the tryout camp, Pop told me that if I cracked the line-up the following spring, I would be awarded with a full scholarship. And that's precisely what I did!

Majoring in Physical Education, I took a physical fitness course in my sophomore year that changed my approach to baseball. For the first time in my life I learned about the proper use of weight training. Armed with my new understanding, I began building, shaping, and strengthening my body.

By my junior season, I no longer looked like the tall, scrawny kid that had come to A & M fighting for a scholarship. Besides adding about ten pounds of muscle that year, I also enjoyed a late growth spurt, running my height up to six feet and three inches. Moreover, I had strengthened my knee enough not to have to wear my cumbersome brace. As a result, scouts once again began turning out to watch me play.

All was going well with the team. Costa had put together a talented and cohesive group of athletes. Even though I led the team in almost all offensive categories—most doubles, most RBIs, most home runs, slugging percentage—we were far from a one-man team. Our shortstop, Leon McRae, led us in hitting with a .404 average, followed by Waylon Winton (.382) at first base, and Joseph Hicks (.381) at third.

Sophomore pitcher Charles Grimsley posted a 7–0 win/loss record with a 2.26 earned run average (ERA, the average number of runs a pitcher allows in nine innings). Clarence Gibby won 8 out of 10 and Joseph Tolliver captured 4 out of 5.

Despite our winning season, we were still left to sneak up on some of the top programs in the nation. During that junior year, Pop had been able to arrange a doubleheader with his good friend Ron Frazier and his top-ranked University of Miami Hurricanes. Playing Frazier's team was like a trip to the World Series. My teammates and I began looking forward to it the minute Pop announced that we would be playing them. It was one of the few games that Pop, a world-class motivator, had to do nothing to get us ready for. His mandatory classroom attendance policy was a small trade-off for the opportunity to play against the Hurricanes.

Never in my life had I been as excited as when we played Miami. Judging by the inspired manner in which they performed, neither had my teammates. We swept Miami in that doubleheader, making national news! Every collegiate baseball fan coast to coast was asking, "Who is Florida A & M?"

I'll never forget how angry Ron Frazier was after that pair of games, which he was probably looking at as practice sessions but which had turned into disasters for him. Taking a kind of a drill sergeant approach with his players, Frazier was screaming and yelling at them. He had them running sprints and laps. He frightened them to death of ever losing again. I think Frazier kept those guys there for thirty minutes, drilling into their heads never to let down for any team again.

But one thing Frazier failed to realize was that his team didn't lose to a bunch of chumps. We were one fine team. We just weren't getting any respect. But even after beating Miami so soundly, we still didn't get any respect. Like Frazier, the pollsters must have believed that Miami, who went on to win the national championship that season, had just a bad day in losing those two games to us.

The education I received at A & M went far beyond the walls of the school's formal classrooms. What I learned through my travels with the team taught me more than I could ever learn from a book. On a trip to Valdosta, Georgia, to play Valdosta State, I learned one of the most important lessons of my life.

Valdosta had an all-white team. That didn't matter to me, of course, and I couldn't see how that would matter to anyone else. Especially during our early spring schedule, when the teams from up north would barnstorm through the area, we played white teams from all over the country, and we never had any problems. But Valdosta was a different story.

The trouble started the minute our bus pulled into their parking lot. The team, the fans, the umps, all of them were gunning for us. Some of the players on our team absolutely refused to accept the racial slurs and innuendoes hurled our way. I was playing in the outfield, and I could see the situation heating up, pitch by pitch, inning by inning. About the fourth inning, a skirmish ignited at second base. Their shortstop threw the ball at the head of our runner sliding into second base. The two players began exchanging words. But both coaches got involved and seemed to calm the matter down.

The next inning it started up again. With cat calls and racial comments coming full force from the opposing bench and stands, one of our players lost his cool and whipped a ball into Valdosta's dugout. Both benches emptied.

As Pop had instructed us to do, I stayed in my position in the outfield until things got out of hand. Then I trotted in to help Pop pull some of the players apart. With a riot on the verge of breaking out, the umps stopped the game and asked us to leave. We climbed aboard our bus and pulled out of town.

It was sad how little respect we were given as a team. We won our conference that year—the eighth time in Pop's career. We had sorely whipped Miami, the number one team in the country and a squad no one had even bruised, but still we didn't get an invitation to the NCAA playoffs. It was a shock for us to hear that Valdosta State did get to play.

I'll always remember the closing speech Coach Kittles gave to the team that season. We were all down. We were confused. We were hurt. We couldn't understand why we had been overlooked.

But Kittles knew. He had been there many times before. He understood racism and had learned how to deal with it. He learned to control his reactions toward it and not to let it control him.

"Boys," he told us, "you have a lot to be proud of. I don't want any of you walking away from this season with your head down. We had a great season. We won our conference. We were the only club in the country to beat Miami, the number one team in the nation, twice.

"No, we didn't get invited to the NCAA tournament. So what? They said we don't have enough pitchers to stand a good chance. Maybe we do and maybe we don't. But right now it doesn't matter. That's just the way that things go.

"Use this moment, boys. Use this moment to reflect on what it takes to be a winner, to rise to the next level. And pray to God that things improve for each one of you, for us as a team, and for this country as a whole."

As he had done his whole life, Pop had used his unique insight to spot the good within the bad. He used our absence from that year's NCAA Tournament to land himself on the following season's committee to pick teams from our area. He also used our resounding defeat of Miami to strengthen his recruiting program and bring even better athletes to A & M. So rewarding were our victories over the Hurricanes that A & M's football and track programs also got a big jolt in hype.

In the long run, everything worked out well that year. The Lord wouldn't let my junior year at A & M end on a sour note. Bill Adair, the Montreal Expos Florida scout, often attended our games, along with scouts from six or seven other clubs. Bill had taken a special interest in me and suggested to the Expos that they draft me the following June, which the team did.

I was chosen in the eleventh round of the 1975 major league draft. I think I would have been taken a lot higher if it had not been for the poor showing that I and my teammates made before Adair and a couple of his colleagues. Sweating profusely under the hot Florida sun, we apparently gave the impression of being lackadaisical as we walked to and from our positions in the field. But we were anything but lazy. As I still do today, we were just trying to conserve energy. Moreover, I did not give the most convincing demonstration of my pro potential that day. I popped up once and struck out twice in three at-bats.

Seven of my A & M teammates were selected in that draft as well.

But being drafted did not mean that I would automatically be signed by the Expos. It was standard procedure for all of their lower draft picks to work out in front of all of the scouts at their Class A facilities in West Palm Beach. They made it clear to me that any potential financial offer would be based on my performance in West Palm.

A few days later I flew to West Palm. All of the Expos top brass were there, including the club's President John McHale, a powerful big league executive and one of the best judges of talent in baseball. I must have done reasonably well, for after the tryout the Expos contacted me with an offer of a $2,000 signing bonus and a chance to play for their Rookie League club in Lethbridge, Alberta.

That night I was on the telephone with my always optimistic uncle John. He strongly recommended that I take the offer. He felt that I all I needed was a fair chance to showcase my wares and I would be on my way to the big leagues.

As always, I decided to pray on it and let the Lord be my guide.

It wasn't the money that made me take the Expos offer. Even back then $2000 wasn't a lot of money. It was the opportunity to play professional baseball that I craved. Leaving A & M after my junior year wasn't easy. But the truth was that I could no longer stay. My heart was no longer in it. It was, and for the next twenty years would be, with the game of baseball.

CHAPTER SIX

A Straight Run to the Bigs

I was thankful to the Lord for being drafted by the Expos and being sent to the Rookie League (called the Pioneer League) in Lethbridge, Alberta. As I had often done, I put my destiny in his hands and played my heart out. It's amazing how much you can accomplish when you trust in the Lord to get you to where you're going.

Lethbridge is a friendly little town nestled away in the majestic Rocky Mountains. Three things stand out in my mind about this town. First, I recall the constant odor given off by a nearby slaughterhouse. I had been around paper mills and pulp factories, and they had given off an awful smell. But that slaughterhouse went far beyond awful. It was disgusting.

The second thing about playing at Lethbridge were the long, long bus rides we had to take to play in other cities. The Pioneer League could easily be renamed the Long, Slow Bus Ride League, and I don't think anyone would have complained. Our nearest opponent in Montana was nine hours away (and Idaho was even further), and the windy mountainous roads we had to take were hazardous and slow.

Third, I vividly recall my roommate, Andy Dyes. He was a real muscular guy who thrived on body-building. He was considered a better prospect than I was and was on the fast track to the major leagues. Unfortunately, some personal problems intervened, and he had to drop out of the game. That often happens in baseball. Players with great physical talent fall prey to situations or distractions outside the playing arena. Whether you make it to the big leagues or not often depends on whether you are able to shield your play on the field from distractions off the diamond. When Andy went down, I was so thankful that I had learned early on to separate the inconveniences of life from my play on the field.

All in all, I was just happy to be playing professional baseball. While at Lethbridge, I broke most of the records that Steve Garvey had established. I led the league in homers with 13 and in hits with 99, and was named the Pioneer League Player of the Year.

When I arrived back in Miami after the season, everyone was glad to see me, especially after hearing how well I had done. My uncle John started what became a tradition: collecting the daily newspapers from the cities I had played in. How he was able to find copies of the Billings newspaper, which listed our stats and gave daily summations of our games, I don't know. But when I arrived home, everybody in my family knew exactly how well I had done.

My uncles were especially proud. I got the sense that vicariously they were living out their dreams of being ballplayers through me. As far as I was concerned, they should feel close to my accomplishments because in my mind they are and always will be a big part of anything good that comes of my life.

Sugar Bo was obviously waiting for me, and I couldn't wait to compare notes with him about all that had happened to me that year. As always, Bo spoke to me straight from the heart. We spent a lot of time hanging around and working out together. I used every opportunity to figure out what I should be preparing myself for and what I could be doing better.

While I was home that first off-season, I also received a call from one of my aunts on my father's side. I've already mentioned how little my father had to do with me. When he returned home on furloughs from the military overseas, I usually visited him, though I was often at a loss for words. I didn't know how he felt about me, and I wasn't clear on how I felt about him. Though I was glad to see him, I often left confused and wondering.

After he retired, my father was around the area a lot more, but nothing seemed to change. We still didn't spend much time together. When we did run into each other, our conversation was politely void of emotion or affection. I always felt like a stranger in his company. I may have been better off not knowing my father at all—with the exception of one important point. For if I had never known him, I would never have had the pleasure of knowing and loving his mother, my grandmother, Martha Dawson.

For everything my father did wrong, my grandmother did right. She loved me with all her heart. I was a priority in her life. I was her grandson, and she was proud of me and adored me, whether her son chose to acknowledge me or not.

As a boy, I often spent weekends with her. I always looked forward to seeing her, especially at Christmas, when she would make sure there were ten to fifteen individually wrapped presents for me under her tree. She was my only true connection with my father, keeping me posted on where he was and what he was doing. She told me about each of his promotions. If it wasn't for her, he might never have come by for a visit.

My aunt's call grieved me deeply, for she told me about the stroke my grandmother had suffered. By the time I knew about it, she was completely bedridden and one of her legs had been amputated. She was gradually slipping away. Most of the time when I stopped by to visit her she was sleeping. At best we talked briefly. I could see she was fighting a losing battle.

A few weeks before I was scheduled to leave for spring training I got a phone call that she had died. The news was hard for me to hear, but I was glad that her suffering was finally over. At her funeral, I began to wonder if I would never hear from any of my father's family again.

But I didn't need to worry. After my grandmother's death, I went by occasionally to visit my grandfather. He was always glad to see me and spent time talking with me. A couple years ago he too had a stroke and died. His sister, my Aunt Florence, and I still talk regularly.

Shortly after my grandmother's passing, I received word from the Expos that because of my accomplishments in my first year in pro ball, they wanted me to begin playing on their AA in Quebec City next season. Initially their suggestion disappointed me. I was looking forward to playing on a regular basis before my family and friends with the Expos A club in nearby West Palm. Sugar Bo, John, and Curtis understood my reasoning, but they made me realize how much a compliment the Expos were paying me by wanting me to play on an AA team.

Quebec City was the coldest place I had ever been in my life. That was the toughest part of playing there. I never seemed to be able to get the chill out of my bones. It even snowed once while we were playing there in May—only the second time in my life I had seen snow.

But snow or no snow, cold or no cold, I was determined to make it to the majors, and I was trusting the Lord to get me there. All I had to do was to give my very best.

As a result, I had a great start that year. I was at the top of the league in batting when Gary Carter of the Expos, who was playing outfield at the time, and Pepper Manqual, the team's starting center fielder, collided while going after the ball. Carter broke his thumb and Manqual injured his shoulder, putting both of them on the disabled list.

Phenoms Ellis Valentine and Gary Roenicke were called to Montreal to replace the pair. That meant that the Denver Rockies, the Expos AAA team, were short of outfielders, and I was called up the next day to join their team. Now I was only one move away from the major leagues! As excited as I was, I hit twelve homers in my first four-teen games. The Expos scouts were soon flying and driving in to take a good look at me.

While at Denver I got to know a fellow player—wild, crazy, and outspoken Warren Cromartie. Cro and I had initially met during the previous spring training and had taken an immediate liking to each other. We were both from the Miami area; our homes were only thirty minutes apart. He had gone to Jackson High School in Liberty City, and we both came from very similar hardworking, blue collar, spiritually based backgrounds. Like me, he had been an all-city high school ball player but hadn't been offered any scholarship from the bigger schools. The University of Miami had offered him free books and board but that was all. He ended up going to Miami Dade Community College instead, where he needed only two years of playing baseball before he was eligible for the draft.

Cro's playing ability had carried him around the world, playing for teams in Venezuela and Anchorage, Alaska. He had been chosen along with a group of other college all-stars to barnstorm their way through Japan. While in Quebec City he had met and married his wife, Carol.

As a Denver Rockie, Cro was switching back and forth between right field and first base. Not blessed with great speed or a powerful arm, he had gotten where he was through determination and hard work. His elevation to the big leagues seemed imminent. Everyone on the team, including Cro, could feel it, and I couldn't be happier for anyone.

Cro did everything he could to encourage me and share with me what he already knew. We became such good friends we soon began calling each other "Homie," short for "homeboy."

In spite of our similar work ethic, background, and approach to playing the game, I feel it was our differences that really drew us to each other. He had an outgoing personality, which I appreciated. He said things that never entered my mind, becoming sort of my alter ego.

For his side, I think my in-depth concentration tickled him. He loved to jerk me around. If he got a smile from me, he knew he had accomplished something of significance. He also did the first, only, and finest impersonation of me I have ever seen.

By the time the Expos called up Cro only a few weeks after I arrived in Denver, I was already conditioned to break into a smile whenever he entered my presence. And Cro was never a man to complain. As with everything else in his life, he simply accepted the situation for what it was and went out to make the best of it. That was his greatest strength.

Because of my impressive stint with Denver, the big club called me up on September 7 as part of the September roster expansion. I got my first big-league hit off of Steve Carlton on September 13 and was invited by the Expos to join them in spring training in 1977, where I won a starting job with the Montreal club.

Through the mid-1970s, major league baseball was the only industry in the United States where a segment of its employees, the players, were unable to move freely between employers. They were denied this constitutional right because of what was commonly referred to as the reserve clause. According to this clause, the owners reserve the rights among themselves to decide who plays where. A player belongs to a club until the manager decides to trade him, release him, or retire him.

Miller and Moss, with the solidarity and support of the players firmly behind them, were determined to change this. In 1975, Dodgers Andy Messersmith and the Orioles Dave McNally challenged the constrictive reserve clause by playing the entire season without a contract. According to the fiery Moss, this would free them from their binding contracts with their clubs. The owners, of course, felt differently.

It all came down to a courtroom battle between the players, represented by the animated Moss and the owners. Moss won the decision in front of arbitrator Peter Seitz, for whom the landmark case was eventually named. That decision was upheld by the Supreme Court of the United States, opening the door for not only Messersmith and McNally to freely negotiate with other clubs, but all major leaguers as well.

When Messersmith decided to challenge the reserve clause, he was one of baseball's best pitchers. His 20–6 record and 2.59 ERA represented some of the top numbers in the National League. Messersmith also led the league in win/loss percentage and pitched for a pennant-winning Dodger team. His victory in Game Two of the National League Championship Series helped Los Angeles play their way into the World Series.

The following year, Messersmith turned in numbers nearly as outstanding, leading the National League in starts, complete games, innings pitches, shutouts, and fewest hits allowed per nine innings pitched. He also finished third in wins (19), third in strikeouts (213), and second in ERA. He was named to the National League All-Star team and won a Golden Glove award.

In a bidding war of unprecedented dimensions, Ted Turner, outspoken and innovative owner of the Braves and hungry for a championship to be brought to Atlanta, outbid several other suitors to land Messersmith's services for $1,750,000, which was to be spread over several years.

Either Messersmith's finest years were behind him once he signed with the Braves or the excitement of challenging the restraining reserve clause had taken the best out of him. His career went rapidly downhill after signing with the Braves. Though he pitched adequately in 1976, with an 11–11 record, the money he was making caused fans and fellow players to expect more out of him. In 1977, injuries kept him from playing at all, and in 1978, he was sold to the New York Yankees. By the following year he had played his way out of the game.

On the other hand, McNally, a competitive left-hander and a hero in Baltimore for many years, was on the downside of his career when he decided to challenge the reserve clause. He had outpitched Don Drysdale in a 1–0 showdown in the fourth game of the 1966 World Series, giving the Orioles their first ever win in the fall classic. Two year later, he won 22 games, and in 1970 he posted 24 victories.

After the Seitz Decision, he signed on with the Expos for the 1976 season. But he finished the season with only three wins in nine decisions and retired immediately thereafter.

But no matter what Messersmith and McNally did after they became free agents, no one can dispute what they did for baseball by having the nerve to try to become free agents.

The battle over the Seitz Decision would not end there, however. The owners were determined not to take the loss sitting down. In an attempt to regain their leverage at the negotiating table, they staged an abortive lockout of spring training camps in 1977. Eventually they returned to the bargaining table, where a compromise was reached.

Both sides agreed to a deal that would allow six-year major league veterans to auction off their services through an annual re-entry draft. As some owners began bidding high salaries for these free agents, the pay scale that other players could expect, especially through arbitration, would be raised substantially as well.

With eleven hard-fought years behind him, Moss resigned at the end of 1976 as general counsel for the Major League Players' Association and went into business representing and negotiating contracts for players.

PART THREE

A Familiar
Yet Foreign Country

CHAPTER SEVEN

Lonely, Then Relief

By the time I landed in the big leagues for good in 1977, baseball was going through a major transition. Because of the newly passed free agency laws, players were jumping from here to there, from team to team, from league to league. Managers were beginning to do the same. All the flux and instability made me nervous. In the long run, however, it was good for the players and for baseball.

The new laws definitely worked for the benefit of the Expos. No longer did the teams that had recently entered into the major leagues, like Montreal, have to elevate their teams slowly into competitiveness through their farm systems and trades. They could buy championship players on the open market.

That is precisely what the Expos did with Dave Cash. For years Dave had played second base for the pennant-winning Philadelphia Phillies. He was one of the first to take advantage of the new laws. His presence added stability to our infield and firm leadership and poise to our clubhouse.

The Expos also traded two pitchers for first baseman Tony Perez. Tony had long been a major cog in Cincinnati's Big Red teams of the 1970s.

Next, the management of the Expos traded catcher Barry Foote to the Phillies to make room for Gary Carter and his powerful bat at the plate. Until that time, Carter had played both the outfield and catcher. But when Ellis Valentine established himself in 1976 as the Expos right fielder of the future, there was no other place for Gary to go—either behind the plate or to another team. In retrospect, the Expos would have been foolish to trade him, but at such a young stage in his career, Carter had yet to prove himself. According to rumors, the club had unsuccessfully tried to peddle Carter and power-hitting third baseman Larry Parrish to a number of clubs.

In one last move to strengthen our club up the middle and to calm and mature our clubhouse, shortstop "Wildhorse" Tim Foli was traded to the San Francisco Giants for steady Chris Speier. Foli, who later accepted Jesus Christ as his Savior, went on to become an essential part of a World Series team in Pittsburgh, leaving behind him a trunkload of legends in Montreal. Before becoming a Christian, Foli's anger as an Expo had often incited the opposing team into a fight, but his teammates refused to run to his aid. It's amazing what one's conversion can do. Almost overnight, Foli went from being hated in Montreal to being loved in Pittsburgh.

Frustrated by their first few years in the league, the Expos management were antsy to do something big by 1977. That's why they had gone after the Speiers, Cashes, and Perezes. That's also why they had fired Gene Mauch in 1975, who hadn't accomplished much, and hired and fired Karl Kuehl and tough-minded Charlie Fox in 1976, before committing to a long-term arrangement with highly successful but controversial manager Dick Williams in 1977. Now they felt that they would be serious contenders in the National League.

Williams had won everywhere he had managed. He had broken a long dry spell for the Boston Red Sox in 1967 when he took them to the World Series during his first big league managing stint. A few years later, he led the Oakland A's dynasty to three consecutive American League pennants from 1971 to 1973.

Dick was known as a take-charge sort of manager. He preferred to have a standard line-up that he used against all types of pitchers and all sorts of teams. He didn't believe in platooning. Though the players seemed to love him because of that, the pitchers feared him. Many thought his knowledge of the pitching end of the game wasn't as well developed as the playing end.

What Williams inherited when spring training opened in 1977 was an established line-up. Carter was behind the plate, Perez at first, Cash at second, Speier at short, and Parrish at third. The outfield was made up of me in center field, Cro in left, and second-year player Valentine in right. This was the team that the Expos felt would bring the first World Series crown to Canada, and they were sure that Williams was the man to get them there.

Cromartie and I were just two of the highly touted "can't miss" athletes to come out of the Miami area. Why so many others didn't make it to the big time, I'm not sure. Maybe it had to do with Miami's slow turn away from segregation, which caused clubs not to give those athletes the chance they deserved. Maybe the Lord was just smiling extra special on Warren and me by guiding us to the Expos, who didn't have to deal with the racial issues of other big league cities.

In Montreal, Cro and I were both being touted as potential National League Rookie of the Year candidates. Ellis Valentine, who was a force to be reckoned with, had used up his eligibility the year before. Though we both had good years, hitting an identical .282, I eventually won out over Warren. My 19 homers set an Expo club record for rookies and my 65 RBIs were fifth on the club behind Perez, Carter, Valentine, and Parrish.

All in all, 1977 was a good year for the Expos. The club won twenty more games than they had the previous year and moved up a notch in the standings. Williams established a consistency and confidence in us that wasn't there before. Carter turned in a sterling year in his first full season behind the plate, leading the league in put-outs and assists. Pitcher Steve Rogers, a real workhorse, won seventeen games and led our team into the post-season. The Expos gained the reputation of being a team to be reckoned with.

O n a personal level, I have to attribute a good portion of my success in my rookie year to the calm and dependable direction of Tony Perez and Dave Cash. I came into camp being touted as the next Gary Maddox, the Phillies' great defensive center fielder. But the truth of the matter was that I was raw in almost every area of my game. I continually made up for my mistakes in center field with my speed. However, I was not getting a good jump on the ball, nor was I adept at charging balls hit in front of me.

By the time the club packed up after spring training and headed north to begin the season, I could see why the club had picked up Perez and Cash. For the rapid-beating hearts of us rookies they were sedatives. From them I learned the value of a daily work schedule.

As the season wore on, I began shagging fly balls by the hour, concentrated on picking up the ball as it left the bat, and charged balls when they were hit to me. I also worked diligently every day on the mechanics of my throwing. I threw every day for twenty minutes, just to enhance my arm strength and perfect the flight of the ball.

Perez and Cash always seemed to know what to say and when to say it. I always felt comfortable around them. Neither of them possessed the condescending attitude that is often flaunted by veterans. There was no "hey rook" this or "hey rook" that. They respected us younger players for the professionals that we were, which made me feel a lot better about myself and my playing ability.

By the end of the season I had even become confident enough to stand my ground with Tony. On one occasion, he accidentally cut in front of me at the batting cage to take his swings during batting practice. Batting practice time is a high commodity to a big leaguer.

Players bounce in and out of the cage in rapid fire motion, trying to get as many swings in as possible before their time runs out.

Everyone was amazed when I jumped in and kicked Tony out of the cage. Such actions were unheard of from a rookie. But that didn't matter to me. Even crazy Cro wouldn't have dared do that. "Man," I remember him saying under his breath to me, "I don't know if you should have done that, Homie. Maybe you just should have let him cut in front of you."

Cro didn't understand that standing my ground with Tony was a major step in my development. To allow myself to be taken advantage of is the same as believing that I didn't belong on the same field as Tony or others like him. Allowing myself to feel second to anyone is not part of my nature. Tony and Dave had taught me that lesson themselves.

But even with the ever-steadying presence of Tony and Dave, I must admit that my first season in Montreal was the loneliest and most painful year of my life. I was okay as long as I was at the ballpark. But as soon as I went home to the four barren, lonely walls of my apartment, I went crazy. I couldn't stop thinking about the game, nor could I stop worrying about being shipped back to the minors. I kept putting too much pressure on myself. I had never felt that way before. I began having trouble breathing and could feel my blood pressure rise. It was horrible. It was then and there that I decided that I needed a companion, someone who would be with me always, someone whom I could take care of and who could take care of me.

Up until that time I had not been much of a ladies' man. Besides, I had just broken up with the first girlfriend whom I had ever cared about. I was so completely devoted to my career on the diamond that I had only dated two other women before her.

When I came home to South Miami after my rookie season, I wasn't actively looking for a wife. But if God had any suggestions, I was more than ready to listen.

Not long after arriving home I received an invitation to attend the annual opening of the Coconut Grove Dinner Theater, a first-class event complete with tuxedos and a ride in a vintage luxury car. Unfortunately, I had no idea whom to ask to go along with me. Since I didn't want to be stuck taking one of my sisters as my date, I started inquiring from some of my friends if they had any suggestions. The name Vanessa Turner came up almost immediately.

Vanessa was a few years younger than me, and I had known her since she was in the tenth grade. She used to come over and have my sisters braid her hair. I had also gotten to know her through one of my buddies, whom she was dating. In fact, I may even have been the reason why she broke up with him, because I think she liked me. We used to kid around with each other back then, though nothing ever came of it.

As I was thinking about asking her to accompany me to the opening of the dinner theater, I made a point of driving by or walking by her parent's home, only a block away from my Mom's house. Often when I drove by she was leaving to attend her classes at Florida International University or to go to work or just to go out. She was always dressed up and looked very pretty. I finally got up the nerve to ask her to go with me.

I didn't know at the time that she had a boyfriend, though things were going nowhere with him and she was losing interest. She accepted my offer. Despite how nervous I felt, we had a good time.

I asked her out a second time, and a third time. It took me until near the end of the second date to hold her hand. By the third date I finally worked up the nerve to kiss her goodnight.

No matter how slow I may have moved in the beginning, once I made a decision after two months of dating her that I wanted to ask her to marry me, I wasted no time. We talked a lot that night about the ins and outs of getting married. I'm not sure if we were in love at the time, but the partnership seemed like a good workable arrangement, and I felt we had the Lord's blessing. The next day I bought her engagement ring and made a trip over to her parent's house to ask her mother for Vanessa's hand in marriage—I was too frightened to ask her father; after all, Vanessa was his baby, and I was afraid he'd say no. To my relief her mother gave us her blessing right away.

I left for spring training a few days later. Even though Vanessa and I had no plans to get married until after the 1978 season, and even though we had no intention of even considering living together until after marriage, I left South Miami that year knowing that I would only have to be alone for one more season. That fact made all the difference in the world to me as I approached the new season.

CHAPTER EIGHT

Lessons

We entered the '78 season with basically the same team as in 1977. Management was willing to wait patiently for Cro, Ellis, Carter, Parrish, and me to mature into the players that they felt we would become, while Perez, Cash, and Speier continued to teach us and lead us in a mature fashion.

Realizing how talented we were, some baseball prognosticators even picked us to win it all that year, unseating the Phillies, who had won the previous two National League Eastern crowns. Unfortunately, that did not happen. We finished in fourth place again, with only one win more than the year before. All we could do was watch the Pittsburgh Pirates and Phils battle it out in one of baseball's fiercest and most exciting pennant races ever.

The Pirates, with a new manager and general manager, were behind the Phils by a good ten games with a month to go in the season. Everyone had written them off, thinking the talented Phils would easily walk away with the crown for the third straight year. But the

Pirates, a crazy bunch at the time, didn't see it that way. Even with only three games left in the season, they still felt that they had a chance.

The Bucs' emotional leader for their heroic comeback was big, bad Dave Parker, their right fielder, a Goliath of a man with an amazing mixture of power, speed, skill, and size. Playing with a football face mask bolted to the side of his batting helmet in order to protect a broken jaw he had sustained in a vicious collision at home plate, the fiery Parker challenged his teammates to an unthought-of level of competitiveness.

My teammates and I could do nothing else except watch and learn, but learn we did. Through playing against Parker and his crazy teammates and watching them play other teams, we began to understand the fire and intensity it took to win. Each one of us was mesmerized by what he saw.

During the off-season, while Parker was signing a highly publicized, multi-year million-dollar-a-season contract, we were left pondering this new standard of excellence. My mind never left the game. I was happy with my .253 batting average, 25 homers, 72 RBIs, and 28 stolen bases in the '78 season. Statistically, we had all had good years. Ellis also hit 25 homers and was tied for the league lead in outfield assists; Cro had 24 homers. Carter and Cash gave sterling performances by leading the league in assists at their positions. Ross Grimsley turned in a 20-win season. But none of us were satisfied with what we had done; we knew we could do better.

The most important event for me during the off-season months was my marriage to Vanessa. After the wedding we started setting up our home, gradually moving her out of her parents' house and into my uncle John's place, where we lived while our new house was being built.

The two off-season events just mentioned revolutionized my life. My marriage to Vanessa stabilized my life while Parker's contract set a new standard for my financial future.

As the next season, the '79 one, wore on, we all felt that we had a better and better chance of passing the Pirates in the standings and potentially beating out the Phils. Like a hungry shark, Manager Williams smelled blood and quickly began to maneuver our many components into the proper arrangement so as to make a run for the pennant. Because of my speed, Dick felt that I would do best as a lead-off hitter. He left me there until mid-June, when he dropped me back down in the batting order. Even though I spent the first two and a half months batting first in the order, I still ended that season with almost one hundred RBIs. We were at the top of our games.

It became a fad that year for some of the better teams to adopt a top-forty hit as their theme song. Early on, we adopted "Ain't No Stoppin' Us Now," by Harold Melvin and The Blue Notes. By the middle of the year, when we got hot and began to climb over opponent after opponent, our song became "Another One Bites The Dust," by Queen. It was an exciting time for us.

But it was a difficult time for Vanessa, and I must admit that I wasn't sensitive to her delicate situation. Breaking into baseball's closed social fraternity is difficult for a player, and even tougher for his wife. Moving to Montreal was Vanessa's first time away from home. Not only was she a new wife but she was also in a foreign country, surrounded by a strange culture and by people she didn't know—and I was on the road half of the time. Initially, she felt comfortable just watching me play on TV and waiting up for me to come home. To my relief, she eventually began to come out of her shell. By the end of the season she knew everyone on the team, knew her way around Montreal, and associated, both at and away from the ball park, with the other wives. As much as anyone, she found herself caught up in the excitement of the pennant race.

Early in the season it looked like it would be a three-team race. But the Phils fell out of contention in early August, leaving only us and Pittsburgh in the running. Going into the final two weeks of the season we were in a dead heat, constantly trading the first two spots in the standings. The most that ever separated us were a few games.

But a unique force emerged in our opponents that none of us had expected. The Pirate's elder statesman and future Hall of Famer, Willie Stargell, began leading the team forward. Not nearly as physically powerful as Parker, whom he had taken under his wing as a son, Stargell led with charisma and wisdom. Halfway through the season the Pirates adopted the song "We Are Family," by Sister Sledge, as their theme song.

Stargell used the stage of baseball to speak of partnership, friendship, and working together for a common cause, and did so with great enthusiasm. As Expos, we had no difficulty thinking about winning a game in the pennant race, but it was hard to envision beating Stargell.

By the time we rolled into Pittsburgh for a crucial series late in September, the usually sparsely filled Three Rivers Stadium was teeming with fans, laughing, dancing, singing, and clapping their hands to the Sister Sledge hit. There was an air in the stadium that I couldn't put a handle on, a movement that I wanted to be a part of but which I had to play against.

Until that series we had been polishing off clubs that were clearly out of the pennant race. However, in Pittsburgh we were playing a team full of seasoned veterans who wanted that pennant worse than we did. The difference between their demeanor and ours was astounding. They seemed to love the pressure. It increased their abilities. For us, it did the opposite.

The Pirates were the only nemesis in 1979 that kept us from winning our first pennant. We just couldn't seem to beat them. Though we were the more physically talented team, their very presence rattled us. They took advantage of our youth. They were never out of sorts or nervous. They were always full of life and confident. These are the qualities they extracted from Stargell.

I learned a lot from Stargell that year. He led as I think God wants us all to lead each other. He was always positive. He saw in each challenge an opportunity. He saw the good in everyone, whether you were on his team or the opposing club. He appreciated the value of everyone around him, fans included.

The one saving grace that enabled us to hold our heads high during the '79 off-season was that we never gave up. Even after the Bucs, led by Stargell's dramatic play, whomped us good in Pittsburgh, we didn't back down or give up; we kept trying and gave our best. We stayed on their tail to the final weekend of the season.

Pittsburgh went on to win the World Series that year in their usual come-from-behind dramatic fashion. They beat the Baltimore Orioles four games to three, but only after dropping three of the first four games to the Birds. Stargell, of course, was their hero, named the Most Valuable Player for the Series. It was his seventh-inning homer that put Pittsburgh out in front for good in the seventh game. We of the Expos consoled ourselves by saying that only one team had been able to beat us, the best team in baseball.

The president of the Expos, the newly appointed John McHale, received most of the credit for our terrific run at the pennant, as well he should have. McHale, the heart and soul of our team, had been around it since its beginning. A Detroit native, he began his baseball career by signing with his hometown Tigers in the early 1940s as a first baseman.

After the 1948 season, McHale retired as player and went to work for the Tigers as their assistant director of scouting. It was in the front office that John found his niche. He was named as the team's general manager at age thirty-five, joined the Milwaukee Braves in 1959, was named as their team president in 1961, and won the job of assistant commissioner of baseball in 1967.

It was while John was working for the commissioner's office and scouting the possibility of an expansion team being granted to

Montreal that he was offered the position as the Expos' first Chief Operating Officer and President. He accepted the club's offer in August of 1968, and since then he has been Mr. Baseball in Montreal.

It was McHale's well-orchestrated moves that enabled our team to jump into the ring of contention in 1979. Everyone in baseball recognized just how wonderful a job John had done. As a result, he was deservedly named as the Canadian Baseball Man of the Year by the combined Toronto and Montreal Baseball Writers Associations.

CHAPTER NINE

A Second Close Season

While the purist American baseball fan was cringing in his box seat with the very thought of a Canadian team winning a pennant and World Series, most baseball authorities were predicting the Montreal Expos to go all the way in 1980.

As one reason for that prediction, many managers and baseball writers were comparing Cro, Ellis, and me to some of the greatest outfielders ever to play the game. They were constantly comparing us to the last great farm system that produced the outfield of the San Francisco Giants: Bobby Bonds, Garry Maddox, and Gary Matthews. We were also mentioned in the same breath with Dwayne Murphy, Tony Armas, and Ricky Henderson in Oakland.

Furthermore, some writers felt that the Phillies were tapped out, for Philadelphia hadn't done much to rejuvenate their aging ball club. And the Pirates seemed on their way out too, for Pittsburgh had decided to stand pat with the team that had taken them to the World Series. On the other hand, we had made massive, aggressive changes.

McHale had signed free agent American League stolen base king Ron LeFlore to play left field and lead off the batting order. That move allowed Cro to move from left field to first base, taking the place of Perez, who had headed off to Boston to join the Red Sox. The club also added zany lefthander Bill Lee. And three youngsters, Scott Sanderson, Dave Palmer, and Bill Gullickson, emerged as good complements to steady Steve Rogers in the pitching rotation. All of us felt it was our turn to win, and I was going to give everything I had to get us there.

By 1980, I had fully begun to come into my own. Remaining consistent with my day-to-day workout routine, I was able to cut down substantially on my strikeouts. In 1978, I struck out 128 times and walked only 30 times. By studying the pitchers, by learning new techniques of approaching at-bats from the veterans, and by just plain hard work, I was able to cut my number of strikeouts in half. I also became more selective and less impulsive at the plate, enabling me to up my number of walks by nearly fifty percent. An adjustment in my batting stance and swing also allowed me to hit for a higher batting average while retaining my power.

I had been studying the pitchers so well and gotten to know myself as a hitter that I was even able to predict to Cro just when and during what pitch I would hit the ball over the fence. I was becoming the complete package I had always wanted to be: offensive dynamo, defensive specialist, and base runner extraordinaire.

The early part of 1980 started off pretty much the same as the '79 season. It looked as if it would be between us, the Phils, and the Pirates. Then the Cardinal's Roy Thomas hit Ellis with a fastball, shattering his cheekbone.

In his previous three full seasons with the Expos, Ellis had a .286 batting average with 71 homers, and he was just coming into his own. In Montreal, he was affectionately referred to as the Canadian Reggie Jackson. But all that ended in one split second in May. He wasn't the same player after his injury.

That injury was similar to the one that had ignited Parker to his phenomenal season in 1978. For some players injuries are a catalyst. For others they are the end to all your hopes and dreams. For us, with one of our big guns out of the line-up, we were fired up to try even harder.

The race for first place stayed close for a long time. About halfway through the season it looked as if Pittsburgh was destined to win it again. Although Stargell was on the disabled list for a good section of the season and the Pirates lost eight consecutive games at home, they still managed to move back into first place.

Almost repeating the previous season, it looked as if the Bucs had put away the Phils in early August by whipping them soundly in an important weekend series. And near the end of the season, in a weekend series between the two teams in Pittsburgh, the Bucs swept the first four games. One game remained in the series, the second half of a Sunday afternoon doubleheader.

Between the two games, fiery and imposing John Wayne look-alike Dallas Green, the Phils' manager, went on a tirade, letting his team know that they were not going to disgrace him or the organization by folding the last game of the series. Green's speech proved to be the turning point in the Phillies' season. The Pirates were eliminated from serious contention. Heading into the home stretch of the season, it was us and the Phils.

But in the end, we weren't able to complete the job. Why? Were we perhaps too young? If we had had just one or two other players, would we have won? I don't know, and I don't think anybody else did either. But there was no doubt in my mind that the morale of our team suffered because the rules and regulations were different for certain players on the club.

Cro more than anybody did a good job poking fun at the double standards apparent that year. Gary Carter was his most convenient prey. Cro was always on his case, impersonating him asking for a day off, imitating our all-star catcher whining about this and about that.

Gary was not nearly as bad as Cro made him out to be. But it was fun watching Cro take off after him. At first Gary didn't take to the ribbing too well, though later I think that he even started to like it. It did loosen him up a lot. Parrish and Speier were always on Carter too.

One occasion during the final days of the pennant race comes to mind. Gary allowed a ball to glance off his glove and roll to the backstop. The official scorer rightly credited Gary with a pass ball, an error. Gary refused to accept the call. He took too much pride in his catching ability and had worked too hard to become the finest backstop in the big leagues not to argue a call like that. So he complained and whined about the call. Behind his back, Parrish, Speier, and Cro were making this horrible clanging noise, impersonating the tin glove they always kidded Carter about having. Later that inning, the three of them started shadow boxing between pitches, impersonating how Gary mishandled the passed ball behind the plate.

A minor league player named Tim Raines was added to our roster after the September call-up that year. Raines was being touted as the next great Expo. The son of a semi-pro baseball player, he shone wherever he went. The more I got to know Tim, the more I realized that he was every bit as crazy as Cro. He was always talking, laughing, and smiling. The youngest of four brothers who always had to fight for attention, he always had something to say.

I'll never forget speaking to the rookie for the first time. He lockered next to me, so I introduced myself to him and offered him my hand.

"You don't remember me, do you?" he asked me after shaking my hand.

"Sure, I do," I replied, caught a bit off guard. "You're Raines. I've seen you around during spring training."

"That's not what I mean," he said.

"What then?" I asked, beginning to get a bit irritated.

"Orlando, 1977."

"Orlando, 1977?" I repeated.

"Orlando, 1977," he said again. "Don't you remember? I asked you for your autograph, and you told me to buzz off."

"What?" I asked with great surprise. I always made it a point to offer autographs and took pride in never turning anyone away.

"I was with my high school baseball team. We had come to watch you guys play the Twins during spring training. You were a rookie, and you refused to sign my glove. Isn't it a coincidence that we're now on the same team?"

I didn't know how to take the kid. One Cro in my life was enough! Then I looked in his locker. I had always made a point of keeping my locker neat. Some of the guys used to razz me about it, saying I spent more time folding my clothes and socks then they did playing ball. One look into Tim's locker told me all that I needed to know about him. He'd only been with the club for two days and already had the dirtiest, messiest locker in the clubhouse. He must have imported junk and dirt to get his cubicle that filthy so fast.

It may be hard to believe, but this man would eventually become one of the closest people to me in my life. It's amazing the wisdom God has, being able to see such perfect matches in such completely different people.

Other than come together better as a team, I don't think that there was much else as individuals we could have done in 1980 to earn a trip to the World Series. Most of the guys turned in career years. Carter drove in 101 runs. I hit .308 with 17 homers and 87 RBIs. I ended up tied for second in the National League in doubles, fourth in runs scored, sixth in batting, seventh in hits, and eighth in slugging percentage. We came within one game of beating the team that won the World Series. But none of that made me feel any better. Maybe in God's mind it just wasn't our time.

A few weeks after the season ended John McHale called. The Expos were interested in making me a million-dollar-a-year ball player. Having only made $22,000 my first year with the team, $60,000 my second, $200,000 in 1980, scheduled to make probably around $400,000 in 1981, and still a few years away from free agency, my agent, Nick Buoniconti, the former all-pro linebacker with the Miami Dolphins who lived only a few miles from my home, was more than interested to hear what they had to say.

A few days after their call, we flew to Montreal. Involved in my first serious contract negotiations, I pretty much left all the work and the talking up to Nick. After all, he was my agent, and that is what I had hired him to do. As I was later to find out, that was probably a big mistake. Moreover, he seemed to get along well with McHale and Expos Owner John Bronfman.

The negotiations seemed to be progressing nicely. The Expos were interested in signing me to a deal similar to Parker's, one that would pay me an average of 1.2 million dollars a year over five years, with a club option year for the same amount. This contract would carry me through the 1986 season. Nick said the contract offered a unique opportunity for me and encouraged me to sign it immediately. So I did. Mistake number two.

I left Montreal the next morning, considering myself an extremely lucky man. Mistake number three.

Once back in Miami, Vanessa and I went out and bought our first home, a four-thousand-square-foot ranch style home in a lavish neighborhood, only about fifteen minutes from where I had grown up.

CHAPTER TEN

One Game Away

We were now entering the era of big league salaries. Radical changes were taking place in the baseball industry. The talk entering the 1981 season was more about money than about the sport. The owners' most recent agreement with the players had run its course. There was a strong odor of a strike in the air.

There is little doubt that money can change a person. While many people think that more money makes things better for you, I feel that unless you have the firm rock of Christ under your feet, money usually changes you for the worse.

In retrospect I can see where my ancestors may have been fortunate to be poor. Not that I would wish being poor and hungry on anyone, but deprivation forced them to go within to seek relief from their pain. There they found Christ. Ever since their arrival in the New World, blacks and their love for Christ had been nearly synonymous. Once freed, they carried that love and understanding of God Almighty into their communities. Not unlike the neighborhood that I was raised in, the church became the centerpiece of those communities, around which their lives revolved.

But with greater freedom came greater wealth. And with greater wealth came a greater desire for the tangible objects of the world. Status, fame, and fortune often became the new gods for blacks —and also the downfall for many.

That is what happened to the black man in the eighties. With million-dollar-a-year athletes leading the way as role models for American black youth, kids began emulating the culture's latest version of success. Somewhere within the world of big cars, drugs, and status, the once proud love of Christ that had been so prevalent within their community got lost.

Thank God, it hadn't got lost in me. Mamma had taught me too well. As if she had seen the day of my temptation coming, she had schooled me over and over about the devils of life and how to protect myself from them. So while dozens of athletes were caught up in this lust for status, I stood my ground, thankful to the Lord that what was happening to them wasn't happening to me.

For two consecutive years our Expo fans had been expecting us to win the World Series. By 1981, they were losing faith in us. The front office, in dire need of keeping the fans in the seats, set out to put a winner on the field in Montreal.

McHale, one the most innovative and brilliant men in baseball, made several decisions in order to make us stronger both in the clubhouse and on the field. He let go of free agent Ron LeFlore, who had led the National League in stolen bases the year before, to make room for Timmy Raines. By May, he had also rid himself of Ellis, trading the disgruntled former superstar to the New York Mets for eventual all-time saves leader Jeff Reardon and Dan Norman, two pitchers he hoped would shore up our shaky bullpen.

Raines proved to be everything that McHale had hoped. One of the fastest players in the league, he was one of only a few players in the organization that I wasn't able to outrun. Having led the American Association the season before with a .354 average, Raines had been named *The Sporting News* Minor League Player of the Year for 1980. Williams immediately installed him at the top of our batting order, where he would get the most at-bats and the most opportunities to steal a base.

But for all his God-given abilities, in the field Timmy was a liability. Jokingly, we called him "Rock"—not because of his finely sculptured physique, but because his hands were like stone. Balls seemed to just ricochet off them as if they were granite. Well aware of his shortcomings as an infielder, McHale intended to convert Timmy from second base to the outfield before calling him up for the '81 season.

The more I got to know him, the more obvious it became that Timmy's firm ego and solid foundation were the result of his fine upbringing. The faith of his parents was as solid as a rock, which would become crucial for him later that year.

It was only natural that Rock (from Sanford, Florida), Cro, and I, three homeboys, started hanging out together. By early in the season, we were best friends. We did almost everything together. Cro coined us "The I–95 Connection."

Since we lockered next to each other, Timmy and I became especially close. He was always joking and jiving around me, even when I was trying to talk seriously to him. He kept me loose and made me laugh, something that a lot of people hadn't been able to do before. After a while I only had to look in his direction and I'd break into a smile.

Even though Dick Williams, our manager, was one of the primary reasons we had made our rapid climb during the previous two seasons, you could sense that the front office was losing patience with him. The 1981 season was his "do or die" season. Too much was at stake with the shrinking gate receipts for them not to go in search of a scapegoat. And in all fairness, McHale had done everything possible to give the Expos the best opportunity money could buy to make our team into a World Series class club.

No one knew what was going to happen to baseball in 1981. Would the players walk out on strike? If so, what would that mean to the season—without a World Series? Would the season be extended? Would any strike be so short that it wouldn't matter? Or would the year be divided into two split seasons, like the ones used in minor leagues?

With his job security hanging over his head, Dick played every game leading up to the date the players' union set for a walkout as if it were the final one in a pennant race. When the union finally called for a strike, our club had a 30–25 record. We were in third place in our division, two and a half games behind second place St. Louis and four games behind Philadelphia.

Rumors about what was happening in the labor negotiations overwhelmed the headlines. According to some reports, the strike would cause the cancellation of the rest of the season. Others said an agreement would be reached almost immediately, and we would soon be playing again. The latter believed that baseball was more of a national monument than a business, but that is certainly not the case. Like everything else in the country, the great game had become a business, a point soundly confirmed by the owners and players dueling that summer.

Like most of the guys on the club, I hung around in Montreal for a few days until it became apparent that a resolution would not be reached in the immediate future. As Vanessa and I took off for Miami, the owners were still attempting to turn the tide on the revolutionary Supreme Court decisions won by Moss, Miller, and the Players Association during the mid-seventies. They wanted a ceiling placed on players' salaries and a "compensation in kind" for players lost by clubs in the annual reentry drafts.

Fifty days later, with both sides severely bloodied financially and with the clubs about to shut down for the season and call for a general layoff of their front office employees, the two sides reached an agreement. The owners lost their fight for a salary cap but won the compensation issue. From that point forward, clubs losing a free agent to another team would be compensated with either a minor leaguer or a major league player chosen from a pool generated from the rosters of all squads.

Accepting a plan drawn up by McHale, the owners then agreed to divide 1981 into two seasons. The results of all the games before the strike constituted the first season; the second season would be made up of the abbreviated number of games scheduled after the strike.

McHale immediately had all my teammates and me report to West Palm for a mini training camp. The camp, he felt, would put us in the best of shape possible to make a strong run at the short season pennant.

We therefore began the second season in better physical shape than anyone else. Dick was still our manager, but only for the next twenty-six games. In another gutsy move, McHale replaced him for the remaining twenty-seven games with Minor League Director Jim Fanning, who inherited a 14–12 record. Personally, I thought our club had lost one of the best men ever to manage in the bigs.

Fanning is one of the nicest men and most enthusiastic persons you will ever meet, but he was no big league manager. I'm sure he was a great director of scouting but that did not qualify someone to manage. I think Jim felt misplaced in his managerial position and as a result was uncomfortable and nervous most of the time.

One incident happened in 1981 that especially illustrates how out of place Jim was as manager. Focusing as intensely as he always did, he got so into one game that he actually ran out onto the field while a game was still in progress to try and help Carter zero in on a foul pop-up. Not only was Jim out of line coming onto the playing surface, but he also ran directly into Gary, who was trying to make the catch. The ball fell out of Carter's glove and onto the Astroturf. Jim's miscue caused us to roll in laughter, though we should have been crying.

None of us ever insulted Jim to his face, or behind his back for that matter. In fact, we avoided talking about the situation as much as possible, just to avoid saying anything negative. We realized that he was simply a victim of circumstance.

Despite his presence, and based mostly on the fact that Steve Rogers got hot at the end of the year, winning four crucial games in a row, we won 16 of our last 27 games, capturing the eastern division crown for the second half of the season. During that time, I was nursing two extremely painful hand injuries, one of them being a tendon completely pulled away from the bone.

I n the revamped playoff format of 1981, I was being touted as the finest all-around player in the game. I hit .302, finished second to Mike Schmidt of the Phillies with 24 homers, stole 26 bases, and handled 35 more defensive chances than anyone else in the league. Even though my hands ached terribly, and even though I entered September hitting .326 but hit only .252 for the last month of the season, there was no way that I was going to pull myself out of the line-up down the pennant stretch.

In the first round of the playoffs we took on Philadelphia, who had won the first half championship. Rogers helped us sweep the first two games of the series, played in Philadelphia, by identical 3–1 scores. The Phils then took the next two games in Montreal, which set up the pitching showdown of the year between our Steve Rogers and the Phils' Steve Carlton. Rogers, who had been with the club since 1973 and had suffered through more losing seasons than all of us combined, was desperate to win. I had never seen him so intense. Not only did he pitch a six-hit shutout and defeat Leftie Carlton for the second straight time, but he also drove in two of our three runs with a pair of hits.

Feeling the pressure of my million-dollar-a-year contract, I found myself trying too hard in the playoffs. And the more I pushed, the worse I got, getting only six hits in twenty at-bats. Fanning said it best when he told that media that I was trying to be more than the eighth of the offense that I was. Carter, however, filled in where I left off, hitting .421 with two homers and six RBIs in the five games.

Only one more team stood between us and our first trip to the World Series, the Los Angeles Dodgers. The Dodgers, a bunch of cagey old veterans who had been together for years, were the National League West's first half champ. In a five-game series, they had defeated the Houston Astros, winners of the second half.

After splitting our first two games in Los Angeles, we split the next two in Montreal. The final game pitted our Ray Burris against the ace of their staff, Fernando Valenzuela. Rogers had already pitched three days earlier and was unavailable as a starter. But he let it be known to Jim that he would gladly go as a relief pitcher if needed.

Early on it looked as if we were going to have our way with Fernando. In the first inning we had runners on first and third with no one out. I batted third in the line-up. Wanting perhaps too much to blow the game wide open, I fixed my usual stare in the direction of the easy-going Fernando. Without an RBI in any of my nine playoff games, I was hungry for a big hit. I felt my fingers grip the bat a little tighter than usual as I worked Valenzuela through the count. Having him where I wanted him, I gazed at him once more, waiting for his next pitch. He threw it directly across the middle of the plate. There's a fine line between a fly out and a home run in this game. I could feel the tension in my body I had been storing up for the last few months as I turned into the pitch. The ball snapped off my bat, but right in the direction of shortstop Bill Russell, who quickly turned it over for a bang, bang, 6–4–3 double play. The run that scored constituted our final run of the season.

Fernando settled down after that inning, and we went into the ninth inning tied 1–1. Though Burris had pitched heroically up to that point, Fanning decided to bring in Rogers for insurance. Steve quickly retired the first two batters. Center fielder Rick Monday then stepped up to the plate. His solo home run off Rogers proved to be the difference.

Unable to score in the ninth off of the crafty Valenzuela and hard-throwing Bob Welch, we lost 2–1. Instead of flying off to meet the Yankees, who had already defeated Milwaukee and Oakland in the playoffs, we headed home.

Los Angeles went on to beat the Yanks four games to two in the World Series. For the third season in a row, the team we had lost out to was the team that won the World Series.

On my end, 1981 had been the finest year of my pro career. Not only was I named *The Sporting News* Player of the Year, but I also finished second in the National League's Most Valuable Player race, falling short only to Mike Schmidt of the Phillies. In addition, I started in my first All-Star game, won my second straight Golden Glove Award, and my second consecutive Silver Bat Award. But I would have traded all those awards for a World Series ring.

Rightfully cited for the difficult decisions he had made during the year—my signing, the shifting of Rock from second base to left, his refusal to trade Steve Rogers, his trading of Valentine, the taking of the team down to West Palm after the strike, and the firing of Dick and the hiring of Fanning—McHale was named as *The Sporting News* Major League Executive of the Year.

CHAPTER ELEVEN

A Friend in Need

In 1982, McHale obtained Al "Scoop" Oliver, formerly of the Pittsburgh Pirates and Texas Rangers, to play first base for us. Ever since the late seventies, Scoop had been the apple of McHale's eye. He was a truly professional hitter and a world class guy. Unselfish in his approach to life as well as the game, he always had a kind word for everyone and was willing to help with a little advice wherever he could. With his addition, Cro was moved out to right field. I was still in center, and everything else remained pretty much the same.

Once Scoop joined the club, he and hitting coach Billy DeMars went to work trying to diagnose the source of the hitting woes that had plagued me at the conclusion of the previous season. Both were confident that my slump had to do with more than just tension. After watching hours and hours of films, they discovered the problem. Scoop summarized it as only he could: "You just forgot there's a right field."

DeMars was more specific. He noted that ever since I had gotten beaned the previous September, I had begun holding my bat further back than usual, probably to enable myself better to get out of the way of oncoming pitches. After the beaning, my first move once a pitch was delivered was to step toward the pitcher. Billy and Scoop suggested that I pull the bat back and then step toward the pitcher. The change made all the difference for me.

Timmy Raines wasn't himself that year. Both Cro and I tried to jar him out of it, but nothing seemed to work. Eventually he stopped hanging out with us altogether. Feeling that everyone has a right to his own privacy and space, we honored his decision. We missed him, but we didn't really worry about him. Shortly into the season, however, Rock's odd behavior came to the attention of the front office when he committed the big league's biggest sin by failing to show for a game.

McHale called him shortly after the game began. Timmy vaguely told him he had overslept because of a stomach flu or something. Suspicious, McHale immediately dispatched the team doctor to see him. Timmy decided to level with the doctor by admitting he had a cocaine habit. Knowing that he needed help, Rock gave the doctor permission to share this information with McHale. The physician did, and the next day Rock was called into McHale's office.

During the meeting, Timmy shared the intimate details of his addiction. Being a young kid from a small town, he felt a need to fit in with some of the older players on the team. He let some of them talk him into doing cocaine. Timmy started using the stuff on a purely experimental basis, but those he was involved with were hard-core users. When he decided it wasn't for him, he tried to quit, but they wouldn't let him. They feared that he might share his knowledge of their drug use with people in the front office.

It's hard for someone who is addicted to a drug to quit unless he has the complete support of everyone around him. These guys just kept bringing the stuff around and talking him into doing more and more, until it finally got the better of him. Realizing that he was letting down his family, his wife and son, many of his teammates, and his friends, he decided to get help.

During this time, McHale proved to be a real friend to Rock. He could have easily thrown him to the media and allowed them to rip him to shreds. But that wasn't McHale's style. He was there for Timmy. After admitting to his addiction, Timmy wanted to go see a psychologist to, as he put it, "see why I was doing this to myself." Not only did McHale arrange for Timmy to see a psychologist, but the busy general manager even drove Rock to his appointments and back.

The first I heard about Timmy's problem was from his wife, Virginia, who asked me to keep an eye on him. Some of the media wondered why I, being as close to Homie as I was, didn't recognize his problem and talk to him about it before it got serious. The truth of the matter is that, having not grown up in a world of drugs, I didn't know anything about the addictive process. I was unable even to recognize he had a problem.

When the news hit about Timmy's addiction, I didn't have to go in search of him. He came looking for me. For the rest of the season, Homie went everywhere I went. In return, I did my best to keep the pressure off him and to help keep him continually focused on the game. During this time, I got to know him even better. It's amazing to me how quickly God can turn a bad situation into a good one.

Also at this time, Tim's parents made more frequent trips to Montreal. The more that I got to know them, the more I understood Homie's attraction to me as kind of a big brother. His father and I were a lot alike—quiet, methodical, religious guys. Timmy could talk to his dad and know that he would be heard without being interrupted.

I considered it a real honor that Homie came to me during this difficult period. I felt bad for him, but I was glad I was the one he had chosen to run to. I was also proud of him and grateful for his friendship. He faced his situation like a man by admitting he had a problem and doing something about it.

Once Timmy admitted that he had a problem, I knew everything would be okay. By taking responsibility for his problem, he was opening the door for the Lord to come in. Far too many people refuse to admit their faults or problems. I wish they knew how difficult it is for the Lord to help anyone until he or she is willing. But Timmy knew that; he can thank his good, firm Christian upbringing for that.

One of the finest gifts I ever received came when Timmy told me that the reason he had chosen to emulate me was because I was his ideal of what a baseball player and a man should be. Tears came to my eyes when he told me this. It's nice when a well-meaning fan compliments you, but that's nothing compared to hearing that one of your own peers feels that way.

The same month I found out about Timmy's addiction, another unusual incident happened to me that changed my life and my relationship with the Expos. One day in June, Jerry White, one of our reserve outfielders and a good friend of mine, and I decided to go shopping at a well-known department store in Montreal called Eatons. Jerry wanted to buy a stroller for his baby girl. Both of us were in a good mood, enjoying our time together, when three men approached us from behind. Each one had a gun in his hand. Two of the men snuck up behind Jerry and me, put their guns to our heads and forced us, face first, into a wall.

"Don't turn around, don't say anything, and put your hands up," the one muttered into my ear.

Though I could feel the cold steel of the man's gun firmly pressed against the back of my neck, I thought one of our teammates or someone we knew was playing a joke on us. Smiling, I started to turn around to see who it was. "I said, 'Don't turn around,'" the voice spat in my ear. "You want to be dead?"

I heard the cocking sound of the gun against my head. This was no joke. Scared and confused, I began to panic a bit. I wanted answers.

"What seems to be the problem?" I asked innocently.

"I told you not to talk. What? Can't you hear?" the voice said. Out of the corner of my eye I could see Jerry. While one of the men had him pinned spread-eagle against a wall, the third man had grabbed the shopping bag out of his hand and was rifling through it. Jerry was starting to get mad. I closed my eyes and prayed.

Just as Jerry reached his boiling point, the man with the shopping bag mumbled, "Oh no!"

"What?" asked the man behind me.

"These aren't the guys," the man with the bag replied, looking at a signed sales receipt from Jerry's credit card. "Do you know who these guys are?"

The men holding Jerry and me in place stepped slowly away from us to join their colleague. Both blushed.

"Ah, ah, ah, ah, we're sorry, gentlemen. We've made a mistake," said the man who had been standing behind me.

Jerry, angry as a bear, turned around and snatched back his shopping bag.

"Ah, we're sorry, but you guys fit the description of two robbery suspects," said the man who had forced Jerry to the wall.

"You mean we're black, right?" said Jerry.

They didn't reply.

"I guess we all look alike, don't we, gentleman?" asked Jerry, waiting for a reply.

The men just lowered their heads and didn't respond.

"Come on, Andre, let's get out of here," Jerry said to me.

I was still in shock. I couldn't believe that a loaded gun had been cocked and pointed at my head for no reason. I couldn't believe that I had almost lost my life simply because I was black.

On that day the Lord had brought me face to face with the greatest of all devils—racism. He let me sense it, smell it, feel it, and taste it, and then he saved me from it. It would be an education I didn't want to remember and yet would never forget. Through that experience I saw in people things that I had never consciously believed existed.

When we went to the park that afternoon, both Jerry and I went directly to McHale's office to report what had happened and to ask his cooperation in trying to extract a public apology from the officers. McHale, whom we both respected greatly, listened intently to what we had to say and promised to take care of the situation. We took him at his word. But as far as we know, he never followed through.

O n the field in 1982, we finished in a disappointing third place with an 86–76 record. I won my third straight Golden Glove Award, was named as a starter for the National League in the All-Star game, and led the league in putouts and total chances. I finished seventh in batting with a .301 average, third in total bases and hits, fourth in runs scored, and eighth in stolen bases with 39; I hit 23 homers and drove in 83 runs.

Off the field, on the advice of his counselor and with the support of McHale and the Expos, Timmy entered a rehab clinic at the end of the season.

The team also offered Carter a new multi-year contract. His former contract had been structured much like the one I signed in 1980. The new contract he signed called for him to make nearly three times as much a year as I did. I was alarmed at first. Not that I was unhappy for Gary; I thought that he deserved the money. He was the finest catcher in the game, both defensively and offensively, and he deserved the increase in pay.

But I didn't feel that I deserved only a third of what he was making. Neither did many of my teammates, all of whom were more than anxious to tell me so. To them I was not only the leader on the ball club but the best player as well.

I refused to let their opinions influence me too severely, however. I didn't want to do anything rash. It's not my style to complain or hold out. I had signed an agreement with the club. Whether it turned out to be a good or bad contract, I am a man of my word. I committed myself to playing to the best of my ability, as I always had, for the money that I had agreed to receive.

I decided to keep my mouth shut and prepare myself to face the continual questioning of the media during the next season. But I did not want them to see how upset I was. I had to keep my mind focused on the game and worry about getting a contract more representative of my abilities when my present deal with the Expos ran out. I knew that my time would come.

Carter's contract wasn't the most alarming news of the off-season. What shocked me far more was seeing my beloved grandmother after I came home. As always, I was anxious to visit her. More than anyone else, I missed seeing her and talking with her face-to-face.

But the grandmother I saw in the fall of '82 was not the same lady that I had left behind the previous spring. She had changed, though I really couldn't tell how. I could just feel it. My mother and uncles thought that I was overreacting. But when you're as close to someone as I was to my grandmother, you can feel a difference when there is one.

The only symptom I could point out was that for the first time since I had known her, she seemed forgetful. She also appeared to drift in and out of listening to me. This bothered me.

I suggested that we take her to see a doctor, but no one else thought that it was necessary. My mother said I was just worried about losing Mamma because she was getting older. Perhaps she was right, but that didn't lessen my concern. Reluctantly, I let the situation be, though that didn't make it any easier on me. Her condition was on my mind much of the time.

CHAPTER TWELVE

The Beginning of the End

There wasn't a day during the '83 season that the discrepancy between my salary and Carter's didn't come up. Knowing that I may have been duped when the Expos set up my five-year contract in late 1980, the media jumped on the story. Unfortunately, while I tried to remain politely silent, most of teammates, especially Cro and Rock, were quick to spout off for me.

Even though they were doing what they thought was best, their actions brought Carter a lot of grief. It wasn't as if he had gone into McHale's office, held a gun to the General Manager's head, and said, "Give me three times as much money a year as Hawk is making." He got what he did because his agent, the famous Dick Moss, had done a better job of negotiating his contract for him than my agent had done for me.

Eventually Cro's repeated flare-ups with our new manager, Bill Virdon, eventually took some of the heat off Gary and me. Cro and Virdon did not get along. Whereas Cro was loud and charismatic, Virdon was quiet; but he had a stare that would make you shake in your cleats.

A lot of what Cro was feeling had to do with his being in the final year of his contract with the Expos. He wanted to remain in Montreal, close to his wife's home and family. The Expos was the only big league team for which Cro had ever played, and it was special to him. No big leaguer dreams of getting to the big leagues and of being traded around from team to team year after year. They dream of starting with one team, playing for a number of years, and then retiring.

Furthermore, the hiring of Virdon didn't come at the best time for Cro. Entering his free agent year, he wanted to have a sensational season that would lead to a big multi-year deal. Unfortunately, with Virdon at the helm, Cro found himself riding the pines much of the year. As a result, 1983 panned out to be his least productive year.

As a team, we claimed our second straight third-place finish, with an 82-80 record.

Even though I was underpaid, I still turned in the finest season of my career. For the second consecutive year I was the runner up in the National League's Most Valuable Player voting, being narrowly outdistanced by Atlanta's Dale Murphy. I led the league in total bases, tied for first in hits, finished second in RBIs and slugging percentage, and third in home runs and runs scored. I won my third straight Silver Bat Award and my third consecutive Golden Glove. I led the National League in putouts and total chances for an outfielder. I started for the National League in the All-Star game for the third straight year. And in my biggest accolade of the year, I was voted by my peers as the Best Player in the Game.

At the conclusion of the season, Cro and the Expos had an amiable parting of the ways. With Bill as their manager, they no longer wanted Homie; and if Cro had to ride the bench like he had in 1983, he no longer wanted to play for them.

So he entered the free agent market shortly after the season. He talked to the San Francisco Giants, the Seattle Mariners, and the Boston Red Sox. Though Cro thoroughly explored his options with the three clubs, he believed that the owners were souring on free agents. The most he was being offered by any of those three clubs was at best half of what he had been making as an Expo.

Cro refused to accept that. So he entered into a contract with Japan's Central League champs, the Yomiuri Giants, who were willing to pay him 2.5 million dollars a season for three years. The Giant's legendary home run king and manager, Sahahto Oh, called him personally with the offer.

During that off-season I had to have surgery on my left knee. But that was not the worst pain I felt after returning to Miami. We faced something far more serious. My grandmother was sick. I, of course, had sensed something wrong the previous off-season when I noticed her being forgetful, but forgetfulness can be caused by many different things, even fatigue.

Now, however, the symptoms were getting worse. The vibrant, charismatic, outgoing mother and grandmother we had all known and loved was becoming unusually quiet, withdrawn, almost aloof. None of the doctors that my family had taken her to see knew what was wrong with her.

Worried over her, my mother had moved Mamma in with her, but she didn't seem to get any better. Sometimes she left the house to go for a walk without letting anyone know, and then she would get lost. At other times, she hid in her room for hours on end.

My uncles and aunts had always seen me as a baby brother. They protected me as if I was one of their own children. Thus, during the season they had shielded me from knowing the severity of my grandmother's condition.

But I could see how terrible things were. I was shocked, scared, worried, and confused. Mamma had changed and withdrawn so much. She didn't even seem like my grandmother anymore. The very parental foundation on which I had built my life was crumbling before my eyes, and I couldn't do anything about it. Here I was, a married, twenty-seven-year-old man, who someday hoped to have children of his own, shaking at the thought of losing his grandmother. It didn't make sense, but then nothing of the heart does. I never prayed longer or harder in my life than when I began praying for her.

We remained as optimistic as we could, but we all knew that something had to be done. She could no longer take care of herself. She needed round-the-clock care. So my mother, uncles, and aunts picked out the best rest home they could find. Though it was a five-hour drive away, it offered the finest facilities that money could buy. I just kept praying and hoping that she would break free from whatever ailment had hold of her.

CHAPTER THIRTEEN

I Want to Quit

O ne of the most difficult things of my life was leaving my grandmother when I went to spring training in 1984. No matter how much I tried to turn her situation over to the Lord, I just couldn't keep from thinking about her.

I called home regularly for status reports, but it appeared as if my prayers weren't making any difference. She wasn't showing any improvement. On the contrary, her condition deteriorated each day. Yet the doctors still had not been able to diagnose what was behind her illness.

I could hear the confusion in her voice when I talked with her on the phone. Other times she seemed completely out of it. It was painful for me to feel her slipping away. I began to wonder if she even remembered who I was.

There was so much that I wanted to share with her, so much that I wanted us to do together. After reserving the first few years of our marriage just for ourselves, Vanessa and I had decided to begin trying to get pregnant. I wanted my children to know their great-grandmother, the most influential person in my life. I also wanted her to see me play in the big leagues.

Mamma's situation became the number one concern in my life. It was always there, just like the pain in my knees, which in 1984 became more real than at any other time in my career. Simple acts like walking up a flight of stairs became painful impossibilities.

At the plate, when I tried to pull the ball, a sharp pain would shoot through the bottom half of my leg. When I tried to go the opposite way, my knee would buckle. Before long, my hands, my stride, my gait, and my shoulders were all out of sync.

The pitchers quickly picked up on my inabilities. Though my batting average hovered only around the .200 mark at the beginning of the season, they offered me no mercy. To them I was still Andre Dawson, voted the top player in baseball.

Sensing my inability to reach a breaking ball away, that's what most of the pitchers threw me. Some even chose to throw directly at my knees, though I admit those pitchers were few and far between—no one in baseball wants to feel responsible ending another player's career.

On the base paths, where I used to be a terror, I could no longer get a jump. It used to take me only three or four strides to get to my fastest pace. But with the way my knees had deteriorated, I was lucky to get into overdrive within thirty strides.

In the field too, I was unusually slow, so I had to play a lot deeper than I liked.

Playing on the rock-hard artificial turf of Olympic Stadium of Montreal and in the cold, damp climate of eastern Canada was the worst thing possible for my knees. I don't think baseball fans understand the effect that serious injuries have on a player's life. If they did, they wouldn't stand for seeing hometown teams being forced to squander their abilities on dangerously hard artificial turf.

Artificial turf was created for one purpose and one purpose only—to make more money for the owners. Artificial turf keeps more games from being rained out since water can be quickly drained away. The fewer the games that are rained out, the fewer doubleheaders the teams are forced to play, the more dates the club actually plays, and the more game receipts for the owners.

By 1984, artificial turf was affecting the careers of players in the National Football League so adversely that the NFL Players Association had, on three occasions, formally asked the Consumer Product Safety Commission to have turf declared a hazardous product. They painted a realistic picture of their plea before the CPSC. Not only do the rock-hard synthetic surfaces cause a significantly higher number of routine injuries, but they bring with them their own brand of ailments.

Staph infections are the biggest culprits. These infections result from the low nitrogen turnover on synthetic turf. Whereas a player's sweat, blood, and saliva are usually broken down quickly on grass, they lay dormant on synthetic surfaces for long periods of time. Then when a player slides along the artificial turf and skins a knee, elbow, or other body part, their wounds pick up germs left behind by other athletes. Many clubs now require their players to scrub down after each game with a special iodine-laden soap to reduce the chance of a staph infection.

Turf toe is also prevalent. This condition, unique to players with continual exposure to turf, is a painful irritation, burning, and chaffing of the big toe, produced from the germs that hide in the synthetic surface.

Fans in general don't understand the incredible pain that many athletes are forced to endure. They forget that their heroes are not supermen; they are human beings, and they feel physical pain as much as the fans do. All they see are the big salaries the athletes make, and they want to see them play even when they shouldn't.

At least, that was my main reason for playing in 1984. From the front office I learned that the owners felt the team would not be competitive enough to make a run at the pennant if I was out of action for the season, so I kept playing. It was a big mistake on my part. Soon the media began insinuating that the Expos had forced me to play that season.

The guys on the club were a lot more sympathetic. Announcer Duke Snider understood all too well what I was going through. His entire career changed drastically when he injured his knee at the age of thirty-one. From that point on he was a mere shadow of his former playing self.

"When Arthur comes to live in your knees," he once told me, using his slang term for arthritis, "he never leaves."

Pete Rose, who had joined our club and who knew I felt caught between a rock and a hard place, pulled me aside and offered me some advice. He told me what Johnny Bench said to the front office of the Cincinnati Reds' Big Red Machine during the later stages of his career; the all-star catcher flat-out refused to catch. "You can get rid of me, you can fire me, you can do whatever you want," Bench had told the Reds' management, "'cause I don't plan to be a cripple when I'm through."

Cro, of course, had his own opinion on my situation. Playing halfway across the world didn't keep him from calling me on a regular basis. Even though he was really lighting up the league, he was still lonely.

After I told him what I was going through with my left knee, he helped lighten my load. With the approach of a stand-up comic, he'd go on and on about what it was like playing in Japan. That man could always make me laugh.

"Homie, you're not going to believe it," he told me once. "They replay tie games over here." He'd also go on about how the Japanese just loved to hate the American players and how the smaller Japanese players, exhausting themselves, worked out almost around the clock to get ready for a game.

It was tough for Cro that first year. But being the optimistic guy that he was, never once did he call me to squeeze some sour grapes about the situation that had forced him to leave North America for Asia. That's not his style.

Cro refused to allow Japanese culture to change him. He was going to be himself no matter where he was. As a result, as fine of a

goodwill ambassador as American baseball could expect, he was hav-
ing a good effect on the way the Japanese approached baseball. That,
I believe, was his calling. I believe that God meant for Cro to go to
Japan to play baseball.

Valuing his opinion as I do, I asked him what he thought I
should do. He advised me to hang it up for the season.

"Homie, you've got to do what's best for you as well as what's
best for the club," he told me. "You aren't helping them hobbling
around out there."

Timmy couldn't help but put his two cents worth in as well.
"Hey Homie," he called to me one day after taking the field during
batting practice. Knowing the obvious pain I was going through, he
approached me with his familiar ear-to-ear grin. "You know what I
was thinking? How about we do a trade?"

"A trade?" I replied.

"Yeah! I'll give you my legs for your legs if you give me your
throwing arm for my throwing arm."

For as long as I had known him, Timmy had one of the weakest throwing arms in the league. "Thanks for the offer," I smiled, shaking my head. "But no, it wouldn't be a fair trade."

No matter how much I tried to make light of it, at age twenty-
eight, I was beginning to feel like an old man. I walked like old Festus
from the TV show *Gunsmoke*. I could barely stand up out of bed in the
morning. I just wanted the pain, confusion, and agony of the situation
to stop.

At the peak of my confusion, I called Vanessa from a hotel room
on the road. I was almost in tears. She had never heard me like
this before. I had always chosen never to let anyone that
close to me but my grandmother. But I was desperate.

She listened patiently as I told her that I was seriously thinking of retiring from the game. I felt sure she would be upset. I thought
she would be concerned about what I would do for a living and how I

would support our family without my hefty salary. I thought she would miss the limelight, the bright lights, and the celebrity status that went along with being the wife of an all-star major leaguer. But her concern was only for me. She didn't care about the money or anything else except me.

That phone call lifted a huge wall that I didn't even know existed between me and Vanessa. I felt loved and comforted and taken care of. I could be weak, and she would be strong for me. I could be frightened, and she would be there for me. That was the first time that I had ever run to her like that, the first time that I ever tested our relationship. In fact, I didn't even know that I was testing our relationship, though I know now that's what I was doing.

Up to that point in my life, with the exception of what I let my grandmother do for me, I had been a caregiver. I had taken care of my brothers and sisters, raising them almost as if they were my own children. While my mother worked down at Toby's Cafeteria, I was the one they came home to each day. I was the one who rounded them up each evening, while my mother was catching the bus home, to feed them and make sure they did their homework.

When I met Vanessa, it was pretty much the same. I took care of her the best and only way I knew how. When we started dating, I didn't give her flowers or write her fancy poems. Rather, I made sure her car was always clean and running well. If something broke, I fixed it.

I was always taking care of someone. That's why I had found it so easy to take care of Timmy Raines in his time of need. It was natural for me.

It occurred to me when I called Vanessa that the reason that I hadn't run to her before was because I had never run to anyone but my grandmother. Yet I couldn't run to her anymore now. Her terrible condition had opened up a door for me with my wife that I didn't even realize needed opening. God had provided me a wife to depend on.

On that day I found out how truly blessed I was to have married Vanessa. She was the strength and the backbone that I lacked that night. The Lord had not deserted me through my grandmother's illness. I discovered it was not my grandmother who had been so great, but her great faith and love that had let the Lord work through her life so freely. I was now finding those same qualities flowing to me through my wife.

My faith grew in leaps and bounds that day. How great and vast and powerful the Lord is. I knew I would never be alone in the world. Not even Mamma's passing would leave me alone. The Lord was with me—He always has been and He always would be.

Vanessa's counsel that night calmed me and helped me get my head back on straight. "Just wait, Pudgy," she said softly.

"What?" I asked.

"Just wait and see what happens," she replied. "You don't have to make any decisions now. Your world isn't going to end today. Give your body the time it needs to heal. You've had pain before and you've always felt better again later. After a while if you still feel the same way, then retire. That's okay with me. All I want you to do is to be happy."

It wasn't what she said that mattered as much as how she said it. After our conversation, I decided to give it a few more months to see if there was any progress.

CHAPTER FOURTEEN

Blessed in Ways
I Had Never Been

H alfway through the '84 season, most of the guys who had made us contenders in previous years had already left or were on their way out. As already mentioned, Cro had opted to take his career to Japan. Ellis had been traded. Perez, Scoop, and Cash were also gone. Rogers was on a rapid decline. Carter had passed his peak and was being shopped around as trade bait.

Their places were filled by names like Doug Flynn, Angel Salazar, Miguel Dilone, and John Wohlford, second stringers from other clubs or home-grown minor leaguers who had managed to make their way onto our fading team. Rose had been added for one reason alone: to try and boost our image. But nothing seemed to work. At best, we were noncontenders. At worst, we were embarrassing.

As a result, the media, used to writing exciting stories about our fighting to bring the first World Series flag to Canada, needed something else to report on. So they chose me. My .230 average over the first three months of the season gave them all the incentive they needed to rip me up. I guess I can understand that. After all, that's part of their job.

But what the media didn't realize was that my lack of production came because of my chronically painful left knee, not because of any lack of effort on my part. Thank God the Expos didn't feel the same way. They were extremely concerned. Never once did they doubt the sincerity of my complaints. They had grown to respect me for my efforts. They sympathized with my situation and authorized a series of tests to determine the nature of my injury.

While Rose was joking with some of our fans before a July 5 game at Olympic Stadium, I was on my way to Columbus, Georgia. Rose talked about how happy he was that Carter had been named as the National League's starting All-Star catcher and that "Eli" Wallach, Rock, and Charlie Lea would be joining him on the same squad. I could think about nothing else but the throbbing pain in my knees.

By that time, since I was no longer able to reach balls that at one time I would have snared easily, I had been moved out of my center field slot and slid over to right field. Rock, because of his speed, was moved over to take my place.

McHale likened me to the marvelous filly Ruffian. "She ran her legs out in a match race," he said. "Like her, Andre wants to barrel ahead; but when he tries, his legs just aren't there."

For a few years, I hoped to become the first man in baseball to steal 40 bases and hit 40 homers in the same season. But no one was talking that way now. For the first time in my life I was beginning to realize how human I was.

But as bad as things looked, on my plane flight to Georgia, true to my upbringing, I kept hoping and praying for a miracle.

Dr. James Andrews was the orthopedic surgeon who examined me. Andrews made a substantial living looking at knees like mine. What he had to offer me that afternoon was a mixture of good and bad. On the bad side, he said that the source of my pain was a half-inch-long bone chip floating around in my knee. But on the good side, he assured me I could continue to play as long as I agreed to take pain medicine and was given an occasional day off.

Andrews' evaluation did more to make my knee feel better than a thousand trips to a physical therapist. Realizing that I was dealing mainly with pain rather than a season-ending or even career-ending situation made all the difference to me. My mind relieved, I could concentrate on playing ball again.

Through Dr. Andrews' orders, I began to test a number of pain relievers. A few seasons before I had started taking Darvocets, and they had helped a lot. I was using them for the first three months of the '84 season as well. I took one about an hour before batting practice, a second one about a half an hour before game time, and a final one around the fourth inning. They usually calmed the pain, but their side effects often bothered me. I would begin to feel dizzy and light-headed, and I would start praying that the symptoms would disappear before we took the field. In most cases they did.

After Andrews examined me, he suggested that I start taking Voltaren. This medication made me feel substantially better. Soon I began hitting again, and by August I was nearly back to full stride. With the truth about my physical condition out in the open and with my hitting picking up again, the media backed off and left me alone.

M y sister Zerelda called me on the road a few days later to tell me that Bo, who had been experiencing some problems with his heart, had suffered life-threatening complications during heart surgery. By the time the news got to me Bo was nearly dead. Apparently the doctors had lost him two or three times on the operating table as they were replacing valves, but had brought him back to life each time.

Since we had an off day coming up in Atlanta, I flew home to see Bo in Intensive Care. It's strange how a person feels at times like that. A whole range of emotions began running through me. I felt scared, numb, optimistic, guilty, solemn, and angry—all at the same time. It's at times like that that we often make our strongest connection with God and feel closest to the Lord. Maybe it's because we need

Him so badly then, or because the immense weight of our own grief causes us to let down our defenses and to allow Him to enter.

I felt very close to God as I walked into Bo's room and stared into the face of a man I had loved but could no longer recognize. His eyes were taped shut. The color of his skin was whitish gray, and he lay so still I thought he was dead already.

The Lord held me up that afternoon and gave me the strength I needed to face Bo. I had been warned that Bo was so weak that he wasn't able to speak. So I sat down beside him, held his hand, and whispered in his ear words that the Lord gave me to say.

"Bo," I said, tears coming to my eyes, "I know you can't talk to me, and that's okay. But if you can hear me, squeeze my hand."

A light touch was all he could muster.

I knew that this might be my last opportunity to see my beloved uncle while he was still alive—a man who had been like a big brother, who had always been there for me, and who had become my close confidante, a man whom I had desperately wanted to mirror with my own life and who, along his brothers, had unselfishly filled the void in my life left by my father.

"Bo," I continued, "I know you never got the chance to see me play. I've always wanted you to see me play. I've wanted that desperately.

"But Bo, I don't know what's happening. I get only bits and pieces of information. I didn't know how serious your condition is. But whatever it is, no matter how bad you may be hurting now, I want you to get through all of this and get better. I want you to see me play, Bo. I want you to see how far your love and your advice over the years have taken me. I know I wouldn't have even gotten out of the neighborhood if it hadn't been for you.

"When you get out of here, Bo— and I know that you will—I promise you can come and live with me, and I'll always take care of you."

His hand squeezed mine again—this time a little harder.

I left Bo that afternoon not knowing whether I would ever see him again. Thanks be to God, Bo did recover, and by September he had moved in with my uncle John, where he decided to stay.

For me, the season ended on a high note. True, even with my strong second half of the season, I wound up posting the worst batting average, .248, of my career and had only 17 home runs, my lowest full season total. Yet, somehow, I felt blessed by what happened in 1984, blessed in ways I had never been touched before.

CHAPTER FIFTEEN

Closing of the Casket

Word about Bo's death reached me at training camp the following spring. Vanessa met me at the ball park in West Palm to tell the news. About two weeks before, Bo had tripped and injured his knee. John had taken him to the hospital to have his injured knee drained. Complications followed. At first, the doctors weren't seriously concerned. After a more thorough check, they discovered one of the valves they replaced in his heart had dislodged and was blocking the flow of blood.

Their alternatives were few. Hoping not lose him, they chose not to operate. By midmorning of the following day, at age forty-two, he had passed away. My family didn't want to upset me, so they didn't contact me until the ordeal was all over.

The reality of his passing didn't hit me until I pulled up in front of my mother's home and saw all the cars. I could no longer contain myself and broke down in tears.

Vanessa was there to comfort me, as were my uncles, mother, and the rest of my family. But the pain wouldn't go away. I was having a very difficult time accepting his death.

In the three-square-block neighborhood where I grew up, everyone knows everybody. The woman who ran the funeral home, Barbara Bain, had been a friend of our family. She knew how close Bo and I had been. So she suggested to my family that I come forward after the memorial service and close Bo's casket, a ceremonial way of saying good-bye.

Thank God Barbara hadn't mentioned that to me earlier. She did so at the last minute, after the family had already gathered at the church. I had no time to think about her request.

"Andre, I have spoken with your family," she whispered to me, "and they thought it would be best if you would come forward after the eulogy to close Bo's casket for all of us."

Vanessa, standing next to me, had tears in her eyes. She looked up at me and squeezed my arm extra hard for support.

"Okay," I said, bowing my head.

I've had the privilege of knowing some fine folks in my life, but I don't think there are any finer people than Theodore Roosevelt Taylor. This man didn't have a selfish bone in his body. My uncle John always said that Bo would give you his last nickel, and it's true. He epitomized all the love a human being could possess. I knew I was going to miss him.

As I stepped out into the aisle to close Bo's casket, I felt as if I had concrete shoes on my feet. My mind kept saying "Go," but my feet kept replying "Stop."

My heart sank as I reached the casket. I braced myself against it for support. I felt my family, my friends, my entire neighborhood watching me. I felt them praying for me. I thank God for their prayers at that moment, for I didn't have the strength within myself to do what I had been asked to do.

I stood there one last time, looking at Bo. I didn't see a dead body before me. I saw memories of Bo, laughing, playing stick ball, talking to me around the batting cage as he shared his tales of the minor leagues. I saw him lying in intensive care. I recalled my promise and how I felt at that time. I remembered how much agony he was in. I also realized that what had happened had been for the best.

I felt as if I had been standing up at the casket for hours when I finally raised my quivering hands up to meet the cold steel of the casket. I slowly closed my eyes as I stood there, praying under my breath, "Lord Jesus, please take care of him now."

A pair of tears bounced off of my cheeks. I opened my eyes to a blurry vision of Bo, the last I would remember of him. When my eyes cleared, I did what the Lord gave me the strength to do. I closed the casket.

CHAPTER SIXTEEN

Contenders Again

During my tenure in Montreal as an Expo, the fans had looked on Gary Carter as Mr. Baseball. Gary loved the attention. Whenever he saw a camera rolling anywhere near him, he was in front of it. The media loved him too. Why not? If you had a deadline to meet and needed a quote or a brief interview, you could always depend on Gary to give you one.

True, it takes all kinds of people to make this world, and I know Gary is a well-meaning Christian. But his limelight-seeking personality backstaged his teammates with the fans.

Though I am not a "rah rah" type of guy and could never offer my teammates a Knute Rockne speech, I lead by example—an attribute that wasn't given its due credit during Gary's tenure in Montreal.

When Gary was traded to the Mets, we received from them four valuable players: hotshot center fielder Herm Winningham, hard-throwing Fred Youmans, steady, young catcher Mike Fitzgerald, and third baseman Hubie Brooks, whom the Expos were planning on converting into a shortstop. With one trade, McHale had nearly rebuilt our entire ball club.

Besides these players, we also acquired former Red Dan Driessen to play first and moved Vance Law, whom we had gotten from the White Sox, to second. Many were hailing our infield of Wallach, Brooks, Law, and Driessen as the finest offensive infield in baseball, capable of hitting over 100 home runs.

Our starting pitching staff that season had been primarily rebuilt from within, with young right-hander Bryn Smith emerging as the ace.

Because of all our changes, we were being picked as the dark horses to win it all in 1984.

To steer us into our new season, Buck Rogers had been promoted from the Expo farm system. As a manager who didn't ask for anything out of the ordinary, Buck had a reputation of being an easy guy to play for. "Just give a hundred percent," was his motto. "You owe it to the fans."

The miracle I had prayed for arrived that season. Tissue had filled in the crack in my bone spur. Though I still wasn't getting the jump I used to have, my knee felt much better. Toward the end of the season, on September 24, I celebrated by hitting three homers and driving in 8 RBIs at Wrigley Field. Two of those homers and six RBIs came in one inning, tying a major league record.

Unfortunately, by that time we were out of the pennant race, well behind the St. Louis Cardinals and the New York Mets, where Carter was turning in a sensational year playing in front of the attentive New York media. They would soon make him into a larger hero than he had been in Canada.

As for our team, at least we were being seen as contenders again, and baseball had once again become more of a team game. Smith checked in with 18 wins. Timmy turned in a .320 average. Wallach hit 22 homers and added 81 RBIs. I had 23 homers and 91 RBIs.

Brooks had the finest year of all, however. Initially a little nervous about being moved to shortstop, he blossomed once he was away from all the flash and glitter of New York.

A little talk that I had with him when he wasn't doing too well early in the season may have helped him.

"Hey, Hube," I said, walking over to him in the clubhouse.

"Listen," I told him after getting his attention. "I know you've been asked to change your position. But don't let that change bother you to the point where it affects you offensively."

Usually a few words of reassurance are all a person needs. In Hubie's case I wanted to help him forget about everything else and remember the game—the same thing Perez and Cash helped me to do when I was a rookie and my uncles had done for me as a youngster.

Hubie was a thirsty man, and he drank up my words as if they were water. Along with the adjustments he was able to make on his own, he drove in more than 100 runs that season.

Oftentimes all a person needs is for someone else to care. When you tell another player something like Perez and Cash said to me as a rookie, you don't usually have to say very much. The person you are talking to already knows both the core of the problem and the likely solution. All you have to do is encourage him or her to separate the difference between the real problem and the confusion being caused by the devils hovering around.

CHAPTER SEVENTEEN

Pre-Collusion

By 1985, what big league owners feared most happened. Egged on by wheeler-dealer owners George Steinbrenner of the New York Yankees and Ted Turner of the Atlanta Braves, players' salaries went through the roof. Not only were the owners offering premier players the big bucks, but they began handing out lucrative, long-term deals to utility players and bench warmers too. Not wanting to be left out in the cold as I had been in 1980, I decided to hunt for a new agent.

Since Nick had advised me to sign my deal with the Expos in 1980, he had done little to monitor my situation. When I called him and he wasn't in, he rarely returned my call. When I underwent surgery during one off-season, it took him over a year to inquire how I was doing.

Even though I'm a compassionate person, when it came to firing Nick, I found it easy. Unable to reach him by phone, I wrote him a nice, personal letter. In it, I clearly and nonjudgmentally stated why I no longer needed his services. Judging by his condescending response to my letter, he was not very happy about being let go.

After cutting Nick loose, I didn't have to go in search of a new agent. I received calls, letters, and recommendations almost daily from the top agents across the country. I had already made up my mind to choose from one of the top four or five agents in the business. Little did I know at the time how important this decision would become later.

I began my search in Pittsburgh, where I interviewed Tom Reich, the first sports agent in baseball. I also examined the Hendrick brothers from Texas and Gerry Kapstein, the outspoken and flamboyant dentist-turned-agent from California. My reaction to them was lukewarm at best.

The last agent I had arranged to see was Dick Moss, the man who had broken the owners' monopolistic stronghold on salaries by winning the precedent-setting Seitz decision in 1975. Indirectly, I had been following his career for years—from Curt Flood, to Messersmith and McNally, to three of his latest biggest clients: Carter, Nolan Ryan, and Steve Rogers.

I discussed Moss with Marvin Miller. "A lot of people don't like him, Andre," Miller told me, "because he's smarter than they are. Don't let that scare you away, though. That's the best attribute he can have as an agent."

Miller went on to rave about Dick's honesty and the great pride he took in watching over both his clients' personal and business interests.

Indirectly, even McHale recommended Dick when he told me in passing that as a general manager he did not like dealing with Moss, but that he would love to have him represent him if he were a player. That recommendation did more to lean me in the direction of Moss than anything else.

After meeting with the others, I flew out to California to meet with Dick. I'm not sure he knew I was considering anyone else, but if he did, he didn't let it bother him. He approached our meeting with the confidence that he had already landed me as a client.

The man I met that afternoon wasn't anything like I expected. I thought I would be greeted by a brash, nail-biting, abrasive type of guy. But Dick is laid back, though direct. He looked me in the eye when he spoke to me, a quality I always appreciate in a person. He was also sincere. His sense of humor made me feel at ease right away, and we hit it off immediately. When our meeting ended, I was convinced that he was the agent for me, and I felt good about my decision.

While I was optimistically looking forward to landing a new multi-year contract, the owners and players' association were doing battle again. The expiration in 1985 of the basic agreement they had reached a number of years earlier renewed their conflict. Once again the owners were demanding the players agree on a salary cap. They also wanted them to agree to limiting salary arbitration procedures, which the owners were blaming for the soaring salaries.

When an agreement wasn't reached, the players expressed their disapproval with the owners' demands by staging a two-day walkout in August.

With neither side wanting a reprisal of the '81 attrition that they had both suffered during the strike, they eventually reached a new basic agreement. The players agreed to extend the eligibility requirement for salary arbitration to three years, while the owners dropped their request for a salary cap and agreed to sweeten their contribution to the players' pension fund. Through the new agreement, a ten-year player could expect to receive $91,000 a year after retirement.

This new basic agreement was slated to run through 1989. The owners, however, developed cold war tactics for doing battle behind the scenes, tactics that eventually affected me directly and led to a situation for which I feel I will forever be remembered.

For one thing, the owners decided informally, but unilaterally, to limit their big league rosters to twenty-four players, down from the acceptable number of twenty-five that had stood for decades.

They also decided to boycott signing each others' free agents as long as the parent club was still interested in retaining the player. That's called collusion. Collusion is defined as a conspiracy, a secret agreement for fraudulent or treacherous purposes. It's sad to see the power that money holds over so many people, especially those who don't have to worry about where they're going to sleep each night or from where their next meal will come

CHAPTER EIGHTEEN

Diagnosis: Alzheimer's

The first thing that I wanted to do after coming home from the '85 season was to drive up and see Mamma. I thought it odd that my family tried to keep me from doing so. Looking back, I realize that they were just trying to save me from being hurt. Against their judgment, Vanessa and I went to visit Mamma. We were planning to spend a few days with her, take her for long walks, bring her some flowers, and just generally enjoy her company.

No one could have prepared me for the sight I saw that afternoon. She had changed so much that I hardly recognized her. At first she was withdrawn and uncharacteristically depressed. After a while she become wildly excitable and paranoid. Worst of all, she no longer recognized me. My heart nearly broke in half when I entered her room, ready to give her a big hug and kiss, and she didn't even know who I was!

I didn't know what to say. I stood there, trying to touch her while she pulled back, scared of me. I could feel Vanessa's hands as they reassuringly gripped my shoulders. She had known what awaited me.

Eventually I sat back in the chair across from Mamma. She wasn't even able to speak to me. At best, all she could do was mutter a few disjointed words.

I felt sorry and scared for her. I wanted to reach out and hold her, to console her like she had done with me so many times in my life. I wanted to hug her and tell her that everything would be all right, but she wouldn't even let me near her.

As sorry as I was for her, I could sense a feeling that I was even more sorry and scared for myself. How could this be happening to a woman who at one time was so strong and so sacred? How could God allow this to go on with someone so close to his heart? I had never, of course, hated God or questioned him before in my life. The confused, bedridden woman before me would never have let me. But now, for the first time in my life, I was questioning God. How could something so horrible be happening to someone so precious?

During that off-season the doctors were finally able to diagnose Mamma's condition. They referred to it as Alzheimer's Disease, a medical condition that can happen to just about anybody between the ages of 40 and 60. The disease was first recorded by a German scientist named Dr. Alois Alzheimer around the turn of the century.

Its chief characteristic is a rapid deterioration of one's mental and physical capabilities. In its later stages, a person can no longer recall important people and events in his or her life. Those who have it also lose their ability to speak clearly or move about with ease. At times, because of their inability to understand their own time and space, they experience frightening confusion and even paranoia.

No one knows for sure what causes Alzheimer's Disease. Some believe that it is caused by an overabundance of protein A–68 in a person's system. Others feel it is caused by a virus. Regardless of its cause, there is no known cure. The doctors told us that the best they could do for Mamma was to watch her diet closely, make sure that she got as much exercise as she would permit, and keep her in familiar—if necessary, hospitalized—surroundings.

Though it may be true that Alzheimer's directly afflicts only older persons, indirectly it affects all of us, robbing us of our parents, our grandparents, our loving uncles and aunts, and forcing us to painfully let go of them before their time, before the Lord calls them to Himself.

Why the Lord had ever let such a terrible thing happen to my beloved grandmother I didn't know. But for the first time in my career, I dreaded going to spring training, because reporting to camp meant leaving Mamma behind. I prayed for her deliverance every day. I knew that the Lord must have a greater purpose for all that was happening. I prayed too for deliverance from some of my own thoughts and sorrow. And I prayed for Mamma's soul and health. I wanted to be there for her the way she had always been there for me. I wanted to take care of her. I felt that it was my place and where the Lord wanted me to be.

Eventually, however, I left for West Palm, but only because I felt deep within my heart that leaving is what Mamma would have wanted me to do.

CHAPTER NINETEEN

Lessons in 1986

U p until my thirty-first birthday, I thought that I had been a good student of life and an obedient listener. I had learned many things and applied what I had been taught. I was soon to learn, however, that life never stops teaching—a fact that usually surfaces when you think you know it all. Many things happened to me in 1986 that proved how little I knew.

To begin with, I always thought I would play out my career as a Montreal Expo. That's how I had dreamed about my career as a kid. I would give my all to one team, and they would reward me by keeping me around until I retired. I wanted to be like Roberto Clemente with the Pirates, Mickey Mantle with the Yankees, or Duke Snider with the Dodgers.

Thus, when Dick Moss began contacting the Expos at the beginning of the '86 season about a new contract, I thought that agreeing on some numbers and the length of the contract would only be a formality. I was the best player on the team and had more seniority than anyone else. I had played faithfully through injuries, batting slumps, and several managerial changes. I was the leader in almost every club offensive statistic and had received more national awards than any other player. Surely the Expos would want to keep me. And since I wanted to stay in Montreal, it made sense to me that we would be able to work out a deal.

Furthermore, I had always found the team executives easy to deal with. Though I had become leery of the way McHale had seemingly failed to pursue our request to look into the police officers' assault of Jerry and me, I still thought highly of him. I appreciated the way he had built up the Expos and the compassion he showed in handling Timmy's addiction.

Even after Dick's initial discussions with McHale, I was still optimistic. We wanted a three-year contract with a raise over the 1.2 million that I would be making in the '86 season. The club was offering a two-year deal, with a cut in pay to a million dollars a season—a ludicrous offer considering what other players were making.

Though Dick was incensed by the early negotiations, I remained open-minded, feeling that such actions were just part of the process of feeling each other out. I was positive we would be able to work something out. Thus I gave Dick permission to continue negotiating with them throughout the season.

It also entered my mind that perhaps the Expos weren't only concerned about what they would have to pay me; Timmy's contract was up as well, and they would also have to negotiate a new one with him. When I talked to Rock about it, I discovered his agent was having the same problem I was. Timmy was scheduled to earn 1.5 million in 1986, and the team was only offering him a raise to 1.6 million over the next three years, numbers far below what had become the norm throughout the league.

After hearing that Timmy was experiencing the same type of give and take, I felt more confident that something would work out for both of us.

The '86 season also taught me things about myself as an athlete. I discovered I was no longer indestructible. Looking back, I think God was allowing life's devils to test me that year, to further build my faith in Him for the uncertain times ahead.

U ntil that season, I had always taken pride in enduring massive amounts of pain. Managers I had played for often looked at me in awe because of the way that I went about playing the game. At times, after seeing me get my knees worked over day in and day out, they suggested I slow down a little. But I took pride in playing my hardest each game.

Such was the philosophy that I had been raised on. Mamma had taught me to believe in the good and to work for your dreams. The key to living a God-filled life is faith, not fear. Fear is the work of the devil. If he begins to control you, then you're serving him. But if you're constantly leading with your faith, you'll always be on the Lord's side.

Early in the '86 season, I experienced, for the first time in my career, an injury that forced me away from the playing field. It began in April during a trip to San Francisco. As usual it was cold at Candlestick Park, and I strained a hamstring extending myself to track down a ball in the outfield. As a result, every day I had to have the hamstring iced and rubbed down.

I went on like this for a few weeks until the hamstring finally pulled as I was trying to beat out an infield single. About two-thirds of the way down the baseline I felt it pop, and I came up lame. Buck pulled me out of the game. The next morning I was placed on the disabled list for the first time in my ten-year, big league career.

My injury caused me concern about my value as a free agent. On the field that year, I had wanted to ring up the largest numbers possible, hoping they would translate into a major financial deal in the off-season. That's why I rushed back from the disabled list after only two weeks. Unfortunately, I reinjured my hamstring and was immediately put back on the shelf.

But Mamma had taught me well. "The Lord," she told me, "never gives you anything that you're incapable of handling." As I lay waiting for my leg to heal, I thought about that often.

I didn't know what God wanted me to learn from this experience, but I knew he had a mission for me. Whatever it was, I was determined to learn what I was supposed to learn and to follow the path He wanted me to take. I prayed for the ability to look beyond my own faults, worries, fears, and concerns to see His desires for me.

At bat as a Chicago Cub

◀ Christmas morning, 1956

My grandmother (Mamma) as I knew
her during my growing-up years ▶

◀ A school
picture
as a
teenager

Mamma with her sons
John and Curtis during
her years with Alzheime

◀ As a member of the Southwest Eagles, my high school baseball team

▲ My extended family. Standing: Uncle Curtis, my wife Vanesa, my sisters Zerelda and Dionne. Seated: my mother Mattie, myself holding my niece Akira, my niece Ayanna.

"Homie" Timothy Raines ▶

▼ At bat as an
Montreal Expo

◀ "Homie"
Warren Cromartie

Official ▶
Red Sox
photo

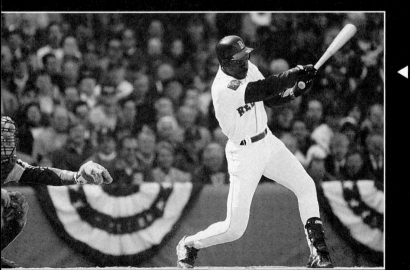

◀ At bat as
a Boston
Red Sox

◄ In honor of Mamma, I have been active in the fight against Alzheimers Disease.

Official ► portrait of Vanessa and me

Between my agent Dick Moss (left) and Player Union Representative Donald Fehr (right)

Vanessa and I at Mamma's grave

Darius and Amber shortly after Amber's birth

Family day at Wrigley Field

CHAPTER TWENTY

Japan Begins to Look Good

By the time I was taken off the disabled list in 1986, I was beginning to realize that I might not always be an Expo. The situation between the team management and me wasn't improving. Though some players with fewer credentials than I had were making up to three times as much as the Expos were offering me, the club seemed unwilling to budge on their offer.

The possibility of leaving Montreal hit home hardest for Vanessa. She was grown comfortable with our life there and didn't want to leave. Besides all the friends she had made, she knew her way around the city. People recognized her as Mrs. Dawson, which made her feel comfortable and bridged the gap between the English we spoke and the French-Canadian language so foreign to us.

During our years in Montreal, Vanessa had even become familiar with the city's better discos. She loves to dance, and she and some of the other wives often went out dancing while we were out of town. The thought of leaving Montreal after it had taken her so long to get used to it scared her.

"What do you mean they're not offering you enough money?" she initially asked me.

Being married to a big league ball player is not the easy life that many people believe it is. The constant travel, change, and lack of security takes its toll on a marriage. It takes a lot of effort on both ends to make the relationship work.

"If you don't play here, where are you going to play, Pudgy? For what team?"

How I loved her, and how I hated to see her suffer. But the honest truth was that I didn't know what was going to happen to us. When I told her that, it certainly didn't calm her fears. She kept worrying and wondering.

Part of her concern had to do with our decision to start a family. Even though we had been trying for about three years, Vanessa hadn't gotten pregnant. That didn't bother me much; I figured that conception is a natural thing and that in time it would happen. But those months when Vanessa didn't conceive were difficult for her. At first she tried to disguise her dissatisfaction so as not to worry me. After awhile, however, she could no longer hide it.

During this time I kept forcing myself to consider the good side of possibly leaving Montreal. I reminded myself I wouldn't have to play in that damp, cold climate on a regular basis anymore. I'd be able to go somewhere where English was the main language. Maybe I would even be able to play closer to home.

Perhaps I could go somewhere where the fans would be more knowledgeable about baseball and be less influenced by the media. In Montreal, since the fans are mostly first generation fans, they accept verbatim the media's interpretation of what's happening with the club, both on and off the field. They don't think for themselves about baseball as they do about hockey, a sport they are more familiar with.

Furthermore, if I left Montreal, I might be able to go to a team where I would no longer have to play on that awful artificial turf. After playing a weekend series in Atlanta, Los Angeles, San Francisco,

Chicago, San Diego, or New York, the six cities in the National League that still sport natural grass, I could always begin to feel the difference in my knees. The pain and swelling started to go down and the spring in my step returned—just in time to head out on the road again to another cheaply carpeted playing surface. My knees ached just thinking about it.

I thank God for friends like Cro and Timmy at a time like this. If it weren't for them, playing would probably have been even more unbearable. Those two were godsends. Just by being themselves, they helped keep me loose.

Timmy buzzed and flew around me every day in the club-house. He was having the season of his life and looking forward to reeling in the contract and security for his family that he deserved to give them.

Some react to pressure by getting tight. Timmy does the opposite; he gets loose. The more pressure, the more jovial the Rock becomes. He was on my case all the time. Thank God! If he hadn't, I would have had a difficult time even living with myself. Most of the time in the club-house he would start sparring with me, jabbing, jiving, and moving, though never getting close enough for me to cuff him.

I remember one time during batting practice that he cuffed me pretty good as he was fooling around. I was casually shagging balls in the outfield, and he was buzzing around me as usual, showing off. In retaliation, I was trying to get his goat by ignoring him as best I could. The less I reacted, the more determined he became. Finally, he came a little too close, tossed out a jab, and cracked me right in the center of my forehead. I saw stars, though all I let him see was the stare. Off he went, hollering and screaming across the playing surface, happy as a pig in slop that he'd landed a good one on me, but scared as a dachshund at a weenie roast that I'd whop him real good for what he had done.

Cro, on the other hand, kept jabbing and juking with me from Japan on a regular basis. I couldn't have asked for a better friend. Ten thousand miles, the International Date Line, and ten-dollar-a-minute calls weren't going to keep Cro away from me. I knew the importance of our friendship to him, and I was reminded of it every time he called.

By his third year in the league the Japanese fans had finally begun to accept him, though it took an extreme measure for them to do so. One night Cro was beaned, knocked out, and carried off the field on a stretcher. Japanese pitchers throw at hitters a lot more than they do here. It's an accepted and applauded part of their arsenal.

Undaunted, Cro returned to the line-up the next day, still slightly dazed from the previous game's episode, and hit a grand slam to win a game. From that point forward he was their number one hero. As he told me, "They're so crazy about me here that I have to be the last one in a movie and the first one out just to keep from getting mobbed."

Fueled by his overwhelming acceptance by the Japanese people, Cro began sharing the finer parts of the Japanese game with me. I think he was trying to relieve me of the pressure I felt because of the bum steer I was getting from the Expos. And he was also trying to convince me join him in Japan.

"They'll pay you the real money that you deserve over here," he told me. "I know how you feel about playing in the States and being loyal to the team. But consider it, Homie."

I must admit I did. Especially early on in my negotiations with the Expos, playing in Japan became a very realistic consideration. There I would easily be offered three to four times as much as the Expos were willing to pay me. I would also have a buddy in Cro, who would help Vanessa and me get settled and established.

Moreover, through what Cro had been able to accomplish as one of the American pioneers of Japanese baseball, I wouldn't have to face all the racial and cultural barriers that he had to take on. He'd already knocked down most of those walls for himself and thus for the rest of us. Because of his success, playing in Japan was becoming an alternative for many players who weren't being offered the money or opportunity they felt they deserved here.

When I discussed the possibility with Vanessa, I was probably premature in doing so.

"Japan? Are you crazy, Pudgy? You want to play in Japan?" she exclaimed.

"Cro says he likes it over there, and they're paying him big money to play," I replied.

"You're crazy! Both of you are crazy! Playing ball in Japan? It's bad enough that we would speak differently from all of the hundreds of millions of people over there, but we'd look different too!"

I decided it was best to drop the topic for a while and let the year unfold as it may.

CHAPTER TWENTY-ONE

The Final
Collusionary-Based Offer

By mid-1986, the fans had grown tired of tales in the press on our rookie first baseman, Andres Galarraga. Vance Law was no longer the player he had once been. Hubie was hurt. Former farmhand Mitch Webster, who had replaced Winningham in center field, was not turning out to be the star the team hoped. Our bench was an embarrassment. Our pitching staff was far from competitive, and the reporters could only write so many features on how the red hot Rock was leading the league in hitting.

So the media decided to write about me—whether I would be traded and to whom. Since the Expos were not denying any of the rumors, being dealt appeared a realistic possibility, which made me uneasy. At first the talk had me being dealt to the New York Yankees or Chicago White Sox. Both clubs were in the pennant races, needed veteran leadership, and were in the American League, which used the designated hitter—all of which were valid reasons for me to be dealt to either club. A lot of the talk focused on my bad knees, that supposedly being the reason why the Expos hadn't already offered me more money.

To me, being traded feels like asking someone to your high school prom. She accepts. You rent a tux, lease a limo to tour her around, make all the proper dinner reservations, purchase the right flowers, show up on time to pick her up, and offer her your best side. Then halfway through the evening she asks you if you would mind spending the remainder of the evening with so and so's date so that she can spend the rest of the evening with someone else.

What are you going to say? Of course you don't want to force someone to stay with you who obviously wants to be with another boy. So you give in, bite your pride, and switch places.

Though being traded is an accepted practice in the big leagues, that doesn't make it a welcome one. In almost every case, no matter who you are, it's embarrassing to be dealt to another club.

I hated my situation, but I bit my tongue and played the good little camper, because doing anything else would have made me look foolish. I decided it best to play along with all the talk about my being traded. When the scuttlebutt was red hot about the White Sox sending Darryl Boston to the Expos for me, one of our ground crew, who came from Chicago, asked me if I wanted to try on his Sox hat.

Playing along, I said, "Sure." So I slipped the cap on my head. The guy laughed, some of my teammates made comments, and a few reporters chimed in.

Somehow word got back to the front office that I was parading around during batting practice with a White Sox hat on. Immediately I was called into the office of Murray Cook, whom McHale had hired as his general manager. He asked me to explain my actions.

"What actions?" I asked, wondering what I had done wrong and why I had been called in to his office in the first place.

"Walking around during batting practice, in front of the media, in front of your fellow teammates, and in front of some of the fans wearing a White Sox hat," he replied.

Obviously, he must have thought that I was mocking the trade rumors or goading the team into trading me away, the exact opposite of what I wanted to happen.

"I didn't mean anything by it," I apologized, and never heard anything else about it.

Later I was able to find out that both clubs had in fact been close to making the deal. Only two aspects of the deal kept it from going through. First, the White Sox didn't like the idea that they'd have to pay me $400,000 for the remaining two months of the season and then stand a good possibility of losing me through free agency. Moreover, a review of the x-rays from my knees apparently scared them away. One surprised White Sox official was later quoted as saying, "They were worse than (Ron) Hassey's," who had long been infamous around the Chicago big league circuit for the painful condition of his knees.

What the Yankees offered I don't know. But as soon as the inter-league trade deadline passed, the Expos intensified their talks about signing me, even though the figures that they brought to the negotiating table hadn't changed much.

Everything came to a climax during the final home stand of the season. By that time the situation was dragging me down. I didn't know where I was going, if I was going, or where I'd be playing next year. The media had been on me the entire season. Some of my teammates, sensing the mockery that had been made of the subject, came to my defense. I just wanted everything to be over with. I wanted my peace of mind back. I wanted baseball to be fun again.

The only pleasant memory I have from that time came from our final trip into Wrigley Field in Chicago. Having learned to take out my frustrations on the ball, I hit a few home runs in one of those games. After returning to my position out in right field, one of the bleacher bums leaned over the outfield screen and said, "Forget those Canadians; we'd love to have you here." The words sounded like music to my ears.

The Expos weren't about to give up on their efforts to re-sign me, however. They knew that was better than losing me through free agency. In an effort to swing a deal before the end of the season, Dick agreed to a final meeting with McHale and team owner Charles Bronfman after one of our last games in Montreal.

Dick sat with Vanessa during the game on that cold September evening. By the time I arrived in Bronfman's box after the game, they were both there.

Bronfman and McHale led off with the same speech that we had been hearing all season, about how in putting together an offer they had taken all angles and situations into consideration. They talked about the condition of my knees, wondering how much longer I would be able to play and how much my knees were already affecting my performance.

"What an exaggeration," I thought. Never once had I gone on the disabled list because of a knee injury. I had taken a lot of pride in my ability to play through the constant pain for the betterment of the team. And as far as actual statistics were concerned, pain or no pain, I was every bit as consistent as I had been after my first two or three years in the league.

They went on to talk about the rising costs of running a baseball team. They insisted Montreal was a small market team and couldn't afford to pay me as much as some of the other teams. Finally they made their pitch: a $400,000 cut in pay, spread over the next two years.

"A cut in pay?" I kept asking myself. "For what? What had I done to deserve a cut in pay? Play hard? Show up every day on time? Lead the team in every offensive category in the history of the club? Be a good leader? Be selected for the All-Star team? Play while I was hurt? Win Golden Gloves? Be voted the finest player in the game? Finish second in the Most Valuable Player voting twice?"

Though I chose to keep my mouth shut, Dick was more than happy to offer his comments. He smelled a rat being waved back and forth in front of his nose.

"Gentlemen, obviously there is going to be a parting of the ways between Andre and the Expos," he started out. "But considering how much he has done for your franchise, I hope that the split can be handled as respectfully as possible. Not only would an amiable break be a fine reflection of the Expos but of Andre as well.

"With that in mind, gentlemen, and in due respect to Andre, I am requesting you to make us an offer that is more representative of the value he has had to your organization. Being well aware of your financial stance in this regard, I promise you, gentlemen, that we will turn it down. I don't think it is fair for Andre to have to enter the free agent market with the embarrassment of your present offer behind him.

"I request you to make us a formal offer of a three-year contract, payable at 1.5 million dollars per season. I promise you, gentlemen, that I will immediately turn it down. I am only requesting this offer so Andre's value on the open market is not tainted by your offer."

Bronfman and McHale nearly laughed in Dick's face. They weren't about to do that.

We showed ourselves out shortly thereafter, leaving the offer that they expected us to come crawling back to still on the table.

PART FOUR

Chicago Dreaming

CHAPTER TWENTY-TWO

My Place in Big League History

Somehow Dick Moss did not seem surprised by what had happened with the Expos. To the contrary, he walked away like a man who had an ace up his sleeve. His swagger and demeanor did more to ease my concern than anything else.

In late fall, sensing that something strange was brewing with the owners, Dick took his top client, Jack Morris, on a shopping trip around the big leagues. Morris, who had played his entire career with the Detroit Tigers, was unquestionably the finest pitcher in baseball. Pitching half of his starts the previous season in a hitter's home run haven, Tiger Stadium, he had posted a 21–8 record with a 3.27 ERA. In addition, he had completed nearly half his thirty-five starts and led the American League with six shutouts.

Dick could have expected to break the bank with Morris. Owners would have been frothing over the opportunity to land such a valuable commodity. All Dick should have had to do was sit back, take phone calls, and compare multi-year, multi-million-dollar bids. His shopping trip should have made Jack the wealthiest pitcher in baseball.

But not in 1986. Things had changed. No longer did the owners appear to be freewheeling, free-spending maniacs. Their behavior changed overnight. While in 1984 they were spending their money as if they couldn't get rid of it fast enough, by 1985, few of the finest free agents available were offered contracts by teams other than their parent clubs. And now, in 1986, potential free agents such as Rock and I were no longer being offered promising multi-year deals at all. Players were fortunate to be given any raise at all. Some, like me, were actually being asked to take substantial pay cuts. So confident were the clubs in their ability to re-sign us at lower wages that they were all but challenging us to try to market our services to other teams.

It was confusing and frustrating time to be a big leaguer or a player's agent. The owners were attempting to flush away all that Dick and Miller and every big league player had fought for and won over the last twenty years.

For the present time, there was nothing Dick or anyone else could do. So he did the best that he could. He shopped Morris around, going from team to team, making a contract presentation to each one. Strange as it may seem, he got no legitimate offers. But he pressed on. He then came to a conclusion that he made public to the country: No one is willing to pay Jack Morris or anyone like him what he is worth, *because the owners had agreed not to do so.* Not only did this hurt us as players; it also struck at the basis of our American free enterprise system. Furthermore, it was against the law. It was unconstitutional!

The Lord has blessed people from many different walks of life with the privilege of being world changers. Some change a condition that has been plaguing their family or an element of their neighborhood for years. Others perform their calling on a more grandiose scale. I believe that Dick fully understood his purpose in life. Blessed with an extreme sensitivity to injustice, this normally laid-back, easy-living individual became incensed at the odor of foul play.

Though he had resigned from his position as the chief counsel for the Players Association after winning the Seitz Decision in 1977,

Dick never gave up the fight for fair play in baseball. As an agent, he was merely changing the angle from which he approached the problem.

The more the owners tried covertly to overturn the decision he had won fairly through the courts, the harder he worked. He knew the owners couldn't be trusted whenever their money was at stake. Unconsciously, he had been preparing his entire life for what he and I would do together in late 1986.

D ick had made some enemies in the fights he had had up to this time. But he had also made a lot of friends, one of them being Dallas Green, general manager of the Chicago Cubs for the previous five years. They weren't buddies, but they were mutual admirers of each other.

Dallas was a straight shooter. He was always up front and told you what he wanted. If he didn't agree with you, he was man enough to accept that. He hated people-pleasers. The no-holds-barred, take-charge job that Dallas had done as the Phillies' manager had not only skyrocketed Philadelphia to a World Series Championship, but had also catapulted him into the limelight.

With the Wrigley estate in desperate tax straits, the heir to the family fortune, Phil Wrigley, had been forced to sell out the Cubs to the billion-dollar conglomerate Chicago Tribune Corporation. By that time, baseball had become big business. It was no longer the hobby of a few wealthy owners, turning a profit from their teams with salaries firmly under their control. It was getting more and more difficult to make a profit. Free agency was part of the reason for that. But also the average American had too many other fine forms of entertainment to stick with a sub-par baseball team. Winning, always the best magnet to draw fans into the ballpark and to their TV screen, became even more important.

When the Tribune Company purchased the Cubs, Stan Cook was the president and chief executive officer of the Tribune Company. He saw Dallas as the premier winner in baseball, a man who could turn things around for the club immediately and who wasn't afraid of using a little muscle to do it. Cook wanted him to come to the Cubs and found a way to lure him away from the Phillies.

The paths of Dick Moss and Dallas Green had crossed several times by 1986, and they had learned to respect each other. Dick telephoned Dallas about my situation during the winter of 1986. He knew that, unlike so many other managers in the game, Dallas could be trusted. Dick was frank with him and told him that he knew about the collusion. For fear of compromising his position with the Tribune Company, Dallas refused to substantiate Dick's claim, but he did not try to hide his knowledge of what was going on either.

By that time, Morris had decided that it would be best for him to bite the bullet and accept the Tiger's unfair offer. But Dick knew that I felt completely different. He knew I could not accept the injustice of the situation. The money I was to be paid was not the most important factor to me. Peace of mind was—I just wanted the game to be fun again.

Moreover, accepting the Expos' offer would have gone against everything that I believed in. It would have compromised my relationship with myself and with my Lord, something far more important to me than anything money could buy. I believe God champions freedom. Without freedom there can be no love; that is, you can never force someone to love you. Love has to come freely from the heart. But baseball was squelching freedom in my heart and in the hearts of many other players and replacing it with slavery. Dick sensed this about me. In our own way, we were both freedom fighters.

Therefore, Dick called Dallas, knowing that the Cubs' general manager would welcome an opportunity to land a player of my caliber. Dick also knew that, because of collusion, Green would not be able to go on the record expressing any true enthusiasm over the possibility of signing me. So acting on his own, Dick arranged to rendezvous with Dallas at an out-of-the-way hotel by O'Hare Airport. So as not to attract any attention, the pair entered the hotel separately through different entrances and individually made their way up to the room.

The meeting didn't last long. Dick made his point that I was available, and for a price that the Cubs could definitely afford. Though Dallas gave Dick the agreed-on company lie that the Cubs already had too many outfielders and that he wasn't interested in trying to make a space in their crowded outfield for me, he also let it be known, in subtle ways that only friends can sense, that he was very interested.

Dick called me shortly after the meeting to make arrangements with Vanessa and me to discuss my situation. When he arrived in Miami a few weeks later, he didn't mention anything about his meeting with Green, but I did sense an air of enthusiasm.

We took a considerable amount of time going over my options. His experience with the Morris situation had confirmed a lot of things for him. As a result, he painted a clear picture for us of what we were up against. It wasn't that clubs didn't want Morris, and it wasn't that they wouldn't want me. The owners had simply gotten together and decided not to make good offers on each other's free agents—their way of bringing down the rising salaries. Even if teams were dying to land a player like me, they couldn't admit it or do much about it.

With that in mind, we began to talk about where I would like to play if not in Montreal. I made it clear to Dick that I wanted to remain in the National League, where I was already familiar with the players, teams, cities, and playing style. I also wanted to stay in the Eastern Division, if possible. And I wanted to play on one of the six teams that still had natural grass on their field: Los Angeles, Atlanta, San Francisco, New York, San Diego, and Chicago.

Of these, I didn't like the atmosphere at Dodger Stadium. It was too Hollywood for me. I didn't like the idea of going out to California and getting mixed up in all that hoopla. I felt the same way about New York, San Diego, and San Francisco.

I liked Atlanta. It was a lot closer to my home, and Fulton County Stadium is a great ball park to play in. But Atlanta played in the National League's Western Division.

Dick had already contacted the Brave's General Manager, Bobby Cox, about whether he'd be interested in potentially signing me. At first Cox, having just signed Dion James, said the Braves' outfield was set. Then, after thinking a bit more, he said nonchalantly that they might be interested if I were willing to sign for somewhere around $500,000 a year. In Dick's opinion, Cox didn't seem sincere enough to be taken seriously.

Chicago, on the other hand, seemed to have everything I was looking for. They, of course, played on grass. They were in the National League's Eastern Division. In my opinion, their fans are the most knowledgeable in baseball, and I liked that. And I had always hit like crazy in Wrigley. In fact, my career batting average for games at Wrigley was around .350. The thought of going to Chicago to play for the Cubs made me excited.

But Dick cautioned me what I was up against. Reality is always tough to take. Because of the collusion, we would probably have to embarrass the Cubs into giving us a contract, which might mean taking a lot less money than what Montreal was offering.

CHAPTER TWENTY-THREE

The Hardest Thing I Ever Did

We got the call about Mamma right after the start of the new year, 1987. Her doctor had requested a conference with all of us as soon as possible. When we arrived, he explained how Mamma's condition had worsened substantially. She had stopped eating, and he had been forced to feed her intravenously. As a result, some of her organs were beginning to shut down.

He made it clear to us that he could keep feeding her intra-venously for as long as her veins would hold up, which, he predicted, would be for no longer than a year. Or, if we decided to take her off the intravenous feedings and let her go in a more dignified fashion, she could last as long as two weeks.

As a family, we decided to take her off the intravenous feed-ings and bring her home. So we called my Aunt Amy Walker, who had a van, obtained her discharge, and took her home with us. We had a hospital bed delivered to my mom's house; it was waiting for us when we arrived. One of us was with her all the time. We took turns sitting with her, bathing her, and feeding her. The most she would eat was hand-fed Jell-O.

Each day I watched her slip away more. She had gone from trying desperately to talk to not being able to say anything. She lost sight in one of her eyes and was beginning to lose vision in the other. Her slow, painful passing was difficult for all of us. I could see the pain, stress, and tension in the faces of everyone in my family.

By the eleventh day, she had curled up into a fetal position. I had had enough. I had seen her suffer too much. Fighting to hold back the tears, I went into one of the back bedrooms in my mom's house. I sat down and cried for a while, stopping to catch my breath before crying some more. Finally, I got down on my knees and prayed to God. Never had I prayed so hard. Never had I wanted an answer so quickly.

"Lord," I cried, "Mamma probably would be better off if she were with you. And as much as I don't want to go through her death now or at any time, I wish you would come and take her."

It was almost as if Mamma and God were waiting until I was willing to let her go. The next morning we received a call that she was dying. Vanessa and I rushed over to my mom's house. As we pulled up, the faces of my family told us all that we needed to: she had already passed on to be with her Lord.

At that moment, even with all of my loving family around me, I felt lonelier than I had ever felt in my life. I felt sad while at the same time relieved. I felt confused while blessed.

Mamma loved me so much that I believe that she had chosen to wait until that time, until I was finally willing to let her go, to die. I also believe she chose to die without my being present, thinking it would be easier on me. She was so close to the Lord Jesus that I believe He would have granted her that wish if she asked Him.

But none of that made it any easier for me. Remembering how much she loved me made her passing harder for me. Through teary eyes, my uncles and aunts (the surrogate parents I had been blessed with) and my own mom kept telling me that it would eventually get easier. However, I hurt so much at the time that I couldn't bring myself to believe them.

When someone dies in our area, he or she is laid out in the church, and the entire neighborhood mourns. Everyone from the neighborhood showed up at the church to express their sympathies to us. Mamma had touched so many lives. Her life had been a blessing. I'm sure the Lord Jesus was proud of her.

The day of her funeral was a day I had been dreading for years. I had a difficult time getting up that morning and getting dressed, knowing I would have to say my final good-byes. How do you say good-bye to someone who was a part of your very being, who meant more to you than you mean to yourself?

I actually felt myself shaking as Vanessa, securely holding onto my arm, walked down our sidewalk to the limousine.

At the church, I was greeted by my family and by Barbara Bain. Barbara spoke for them. "Andre," she said, "your family wonders if you would do the honor of closing your grandmother's casket after the service."

It seemed as if it were only yesterday that she had asked me to do the same for my uncle Bo. My heart fell to my feet. I was having a difficult time just getting myself to the funeral. How could they expect me to be able to muster enough strength to do that?

I looked up. My uncles John and Curtis were there. So was my mom. As they awaited my answer, Vanessa squeezed my arm a little tighter. My eyes met theirs. I knew they were doing this for me. I felt strength and power given to me to answer properly and assented to their request.

I had been to many church services. Mamma had seen to that. But this one seemed the quickest service I had ever been a part of. Everything raced forward until I was called on to do what I had agreed to do.

When the time arrived, I slowly rose to my feet and made my way to her casket. As I looked down on her, I knew that she wanted this for me too. I realized that she knew I had to do this to be able to let her go. But that didn't make it easier.

I bowed my head to look down at her. I knew that I didn't have the strength to do this alone. I took one long, last look at her before closing my eyes.

"Dear God," I prayed silently to myself, "please take good care of her. Please keep her safe and always love her."

I felt my prayer being answered.

"Thank you Jesus," I said again to myself, suddenly finding the strength to close the book of her life on this earth for us all.

CHAPTER TWENTY-FOUR

The Happiest Cheated Man in the World

By the time spring training had opened in 1987, the entire collusion-based drama had thickened substantially. There were still a lot of the top players in the game without a contract. Timmy and I were only two of them. And, according to Dick Moss, the Major League Players' Association was already planning a lawsuit against the owners.

Up until that point, Timmy and his representative had been more aggressive in pursuing other clubs than Dick and I. They had approached every team in the National League. Four of them—Los Angeles, San Diego, Atlanta, and Houston—responded by offering Rock substantial pay cuts. Houston came out with the best offer, a salary about half of what the Expos had offered Rock. He didn't feel good enough about any of the offers to take one.

Timmy and his representative had even contacted all the American League clubs. He was especially interested in playing for the Chicago White Sox, an up-and-coming team. But supposedly they weren't interested in him. According to their newly hired general manager, Larry

Himes—with whom I would unfortunately become very familiar—the club was committed to giving a young outfielder, Ivan Calderon, a chance.

"I don't like to bring in people from other organizations," Himes was quoted as saying, which would turn out to be an outright lie. "You've got to use the homegrown kids."

Realizing the timing of the situation and considering Green's sensitive situation, Dick thought it would be best to sneak up on the Cubs so they wouldn't have an opportunity to brush us off before being able to make our pitch. So Dick and I showed up unannounced at their spring training complex in Arizona.

Unfortunately, on the day we chose to make our assault, Green was out of the office. Oddly, as we found out later, he was meeting with the other general managers, one of the purposes of which was probably to gauge the success and effectiveness of their respective clubs' collusionary actions up to that point and to decide whether their efforts were worth continuing.

When Green came back from his meeting and saw Dick and me strolling around the complex, he was obviously upset. Only a few hours earlier he had been meeting with his comrades from the other clubs. Then, the first thing he noticed upon his return was me, one of the people he wasn't supposed to be speaking with, traipsing openly about his spring training complex.

All of this was part of Dick's strategy. His aim was not to put Dallas in any predicament. It was purely coincidental that the day he had chosen for our visit was the same day as the meeting of the general managers. But Dick did want everyone to know that we were there. He wanted the media to know so that the fans would know. He wanted my contact with the club to become a public issue. That would be essential for our next step, for it would make it much more difficult for the Cubs, with the media and fans now involved, to stick to their collusionary line and turn us down.

After Dallas gave us a piece of his mind, which we had expected, we got down to business. We were more than prepared for what we had to do. Dallas wasn't. Dick took a contract our of his briefcase and handed it to Dallas. A space had been left open in regards to how much the Cubs would have to pay me. Green noticed this immediately. A sly smile appeared across his face. Instantly, Dick knew what he was thinking: Green thought that what we were doing was some sort of ploy.

Dick reassured him otherwise. "This is no joke," he said. "Andre really wants to play for the Cubs, and he will do so for any salary that is fair. That's why we left that section of the contract blank. Feel free to fill in your own numbers.

"All we ask," he continued, "is that if you are interested, you get back to us within twenty-four hours. After that time we will start entertaining offers from other clubs."

I can't describe for you the feeling of elation I experienced as we walked out of Green's office that afternoon. Whether he bit on our offer or not, I had taken back control of my own life. I could feel Mamma next to me throughout the entire ordeal, and I knew that she had played a big part in what we were doing.

With the media hounding him from all sides, it didn't take Green long to get back to us. First he called Dick. Dick then called me to let me know that the Cubs were going to be making me an offer. I didn't really know what to expect. In our discussions Dick felt that they might offer me as much as seven or eight hundred thousand dollars guaranteed, plus incentives. For my part, I was just hoping they wouldn't offer me the major league minimum, which at that time was comparable to what I made in my second year in the big leagues.

Green was nervous when he called. I expected the worst.

"Andre," he began, "we have gone over your situation in great detail and we would like to make you an offer. Please be aware, though," he stressed, "that the offer I am about to make is the best we can do."

Green offered me a guaranteed $500,000 salary, half of what the Expos were offering, plus a $150,000 bonus if I didn't end up on the disabled list before the All-Star break, and a $50,000 bonus if I made the All-Star team.

I thought about their offer. I thought about being one of the top players in baseball, yet possibly receiving the second lowest salary on a team that finished thirty-seven games out of first place the previous season. I thought about how much I loved playing in Wrigley Field. I remembered how good my knees felt after playing there. I thought about the fans, the best in baseball. I thought about going back to Montreal, bowing down to their offer, and about how they were playing me for a fool. I reflected on how a dollar figure could not be put on the value of my career, my pride, and my faith to follow the calling of the Lord where I felt that he wanted me to go. I thought about my grandmother and asked myself what she would do in the same situation. Would she sell herself out or follow her heart? I didn't even have to wait for an answer. I knew what I needed to do, and I knew what I wanted to do.

"Okay, Mr. Green," I said, hesitating a moment. There was absolute silence on his end. I wasn't sure if that was good or bad. "We have a deal."

I expected him to lose control with excitement, but Green showed little emotion. "Okay, Andre," he said somewhat hesitantly, as if my acceptance had taken him by surprise. "Well, ummm, I'm going to have to check with our attorney and get back to you."

I wondered what he meant. Did he have to discuss what to do with the guys he had been meeting with the previous day?

The half hour that I waited for him to call back was the longest of my life. All kinds of thoughts were running through my mind. Why did he feel the need to go running off? Would he back out? Boy, would that be terrible, to accept their sub-par offer and then to have them renege! How embarrassing! Well, at least they hadn't offered me the minimum. But then what they were offering me wasn't any bed of roses either, especially when I had been realistically expecting to earn somewhere around six times as much for the next several years.

I did a lot of praying during that time too. I prayed to Jesus. I knew He would take care of me as He always had.

"Your will be done," I kept saying.

I talked to Mamma too. I asked her all the questions I would have asked her if she were there. I felt her presence around me. I felt it steadying me, as if to say everything would be okay. It was then that the phone rang. I knew who it was.

"Hello," I said.

It was Green. Contrary to our conversation shortly before, he sounded happy, at ease.

"Andre," he said. "Welcome aboard."

I was a Chicago Cub! I wanted to jump, I wanted to scream. Vanessa was there. She smiled and hugged me as I smiled back.

In my exhilaration, I closed my eyes as Green continued to speak to me. I heard all that I had needed to hear. I thanked Jesus and I thanked Mamma for being there for me, for comforting me and directing me and never leaving my side.

I was the happiest cheated man in the world.

CHAPTER TWENTY-FIVE

Died and Gone to Heaven

While long lines of Cubbie fans, excited by the news of my signing, were waiting outside the ticket window at Wrigley Field, my new teammates were giving me a standing ovation as I walked into the clubhouse for the first time. All of them were talking about how my signing significantly upped the Cubs' chances for a pennant.

"I think he'll make us a contender," said second baseman Manny Trillo, with whom I had played a season in Montreal. "He's quiet, but he's a team leader. We've all got to be excited about getting a player like that."

"I jumped in the air when I heard it," added left-handed pitcher Steve Trout. "I'll have to give Dallas a hug when I see him."

Even the younger outfielders, such as Thad Bosley, who had been in the running for a starting position until my signing, expressed how happy he was that I was joining the club. "If they play me, I know I can play," Bosley remarked. "But if they want me to sit on the bench and have Dawson play every day, I don't have any problem with that.

The most important thing is to win. Everybody will be happy, and everybody will benefit."

Dave Martinez found himself in the same position as Bosley. "To me," he said, "it means the team has picked up a great player. All the rest of us have to do is worry about going hard every day. I don't think this will discourage anyone."

Even the media was excited. Reporters were running all over the clubhouse with smiles on their faces, getting reactions to my signing.

Our manager Gene Michael was also elated. "He can hit third, fourth, or fifth," I overheard him saying about me. "He's one of those kind of guys."

Dallas had told me to take my time settling in, to get used to the team and the surroundings, to take batting practice, and to get in shape before joining the team, who were already playing exhibition games.

But feeling as if I had died and gone to heaven, I was too anxious to wait. I decided to jump right in.

The reception that I received was overwhelming. I thanked God for that. I knew that Mamma was watching me as well. In my mind I thanked her regularly for the part she had played in my coming to Chicago. I thanked her for the joy in my heart and for easing the pain in my soul. How could I ever have thought that her passing would mean losing her? I realized that my relationship hadn't ended. It had only changed.

It was then that I decided to do for her what I had never done for anyone else. I would dedicate my efforts during the '87 season to her.

This may sound odd, but that was a big event for me. Until then, I had always set what I thought were realistically attainable goals, approaching the game in the same manner that most businesses approach their bottom lines. I had never made an emotional decision about my approach to the game.

I thought that this rational approach had been the reason for my success. I was about to discover how wrong I was.

CHAPTER TWENTY-SIX

M.V.P.

During my growing-up years, as I cared for and nurtured my brothers and sisters, I had learned to give love. But I was so busy giving love that I didn't have much time to learn how to accept it. It's not that I don't feel good when someone says something nice to me, because I feel great. But I usually have a hard time graciously accepting a compliment.

That's why it was so difficult for me publicly to acknowledge the Cubbie fans' show of affection. Feeling awkward and clumsy, I tried to show my appreciation by hitting home runs for them, driving in runs, making great catches, and stealing bases.

Initially, I tried too hard. At the beginning of the season, I couldn't hit anything. My problem was all in my head. Everything was too good to be true, especially the Cubbie fans. They studied the game inside and out. I could talk, mix, and have a relationship with them, something I had been unable to do in Montreal. They respected me whether I was doing well or badly. And they had hit me in my weakest spot, my ability to accept love. I was overwhelmed. I never felt so good about myself. I never felt so loved.

During that time, I kept talking in my mind to my grand-mother. I felt her there with me all the time. I knew she hadn't left me. I said to her continually, "If you're there, if you hear me, let me know."

I could feel Mamma constantly reassuring me of her presence through the Cub fans. It was like 37,000 living, breathing versions of my grandmother filling the stands every time we played at Wrigley.

The fans' affection for me did a lot for my teammates as well. A tremendous camaraderie began to build among us. Their enthusiasm was contagious and swept over each one of us like a tidal wave. We did every-thing as a team, including going on hitting streaks and surviving slumps. In fact, until our first trip into St. Louis that season, almost all of us were slumping. I hadn't had a hit in ten times at the plate, but I broke out of my slump with a game-winning grand slam against the Cardinals. We started playing and hitting together as a team shortly thereafter.

The first time we played in Montreal that season, I was met by a round of jeers and boos. In their defense, I admit that the Expo fans, overly influenced by the media, were convinced I was the bad guy. Yet I was the one the club tried to cheat through collusion. A scene like that would have never happened in a baseball town like Chicago. The fans there would have been too wise to believe what the media that covered the Expos were pushing down the throats of their readers.

The Expos were pretty much the same team that they had been the previous season, except that Timmy had not yet rejoined them. In spite of his leading the National League in batting and runs scored in 1986, he had been unable to get as good an offer from another club as he got from the Expos. So he met secretly with Bronfman, who increased his offer a bit, and Timmy re-signed with Montreal. But because he had waited so long, he wasn't eligible to return to the team until May 1.

It was probably better that way anyway. I wouldn't have wanted him to suffer through what I did to the Expos that weekend by going 7-for-12, with two homers, two doubles, and six runs scored.

The next weekend in Chicago, on April 29, I went 5-for-5 against the Giants, hitting for the cycle—the first time a Cubbie had accomplished that feat since Ivan DeJesus in 1980. Going into my last at-bat in that game, I had already hit two singles, one double, and a home run. All that stood between me and the cycle was the elusive triple.

The fans at Wrigley, as was becoming a tradition by then, were all on their feet when I stepped to the plate for my at-bat, this one coming with two outs in the ninth inning. None of them wanted to see me hit a homer. They wanted a three-bagger.

Frank DePino, one of our left-handed relievers and a new good friend of mine, spoke to me as I made my way out of the dugout. "I know you," he said with a wink. "You're going to hit a flare to right and dig for three."

Mike LaCoss was pitching for the Giants that afternoon. He got two quick strikes on me. Yet the Cubbie fans never lost faith. They cheered louder and louder, encouraging me more and more. I couldn't believe how much they believed in me. In my heart, there was no way I was going to let them down.

LaCoss's next pitch was the one I was waiting for. I did exactly as Frank said I would. I hit a flare to right and dug for three. The place went wild as I slid safely into third base. It was during that weekend that the media realized the connection between the fans and me was more than just a passing fancy. In fact, there were so many reporters packed in around my locker after the game that Shawon Dunston, our good-humored young shortstop, couldn't get to his locker.

"I expect you all to be back here tomorrow when I hit a three-run homer," he said to them with a sly smile.

Even when we fell out of first place after leading the pack for the first few months, we were still in the pennant race in July. By that time I had become a marked man.

G oing into a July series against the Padres at Wrigley, I'd already hit six homers off the San Diego pitching staff during the season. San Diego manager fiery Larry Bowa was quoted as saying that his pitching staff would have to do a better job of backing me off the plate. In baseball terms I knew what that meant. Bowa was going to tell his pitchers to do a little head hunting and I would be the prey.

Right-hander Eric Show, a sinker ball/fastball pitcher, was the ace and veteran of their starting staff at the time. Someone had to set an example for the rest of the Padre pitching staff, and I believe Bowa had chosen Show to be the man.

Eric had manhandled me pretty well up until 1987. In fact, I was hitting only .091 lifetime off him coming into the '87 season. But in our most recent trip to San Diego I had hit a homer off him early in a game and followed that up by knocking him out of the game with a base hit.

The first time I faced him on July 7, I took him deep. In my second appearance, he decided to make an example of me.

A batter can pick up the movement on a straight fastball from the time it leaves the pitcher's hand. But with the brand of sinking fastball that Show throws, it's often impossible to pick it up until it's too late.

That's what happened with Show's first pitch to me in my second at-bat. I never really saw the ball leave his hand. The next thing I knew, I was lying facedown in the dirt. My head was throbbing with the impact of a thousand sonic booms.

Only halfway conscious, I wasn't aware of what was going on in the field. Pitcher Rick Sutcliffe, one of the toughest competitors I've ever known, charged the mound in my defense, and the rest of the team followed closely behind him.

Rick's attack caught the Padres by surprise. In fact, the only thing that kept Show from getting blindsided by Sutcliffe was the quick reaction of an alert John Kruk, the San Diego first baseman, who grabbed Rick just before he got to Eric. It took most of the Padres and all of the umpires to keep Sutcliffe from breaking out of Kruk's grasp.

As all of this was going on, I could hear Leon Durham, our young first baseman, speak to another of my teammates who was standing over me. "It's a shame we're going through this at all," he said, with a touch of disgust in his voice. "We're supposed to be out here enjoying the game. But look at the guy's face."

He meant my face. Up until that time, I hadn't fully realized the extent of my injury. But his comment put everything in perspective. In seconds I found myself on my feet, with only one goal in my mind: to get Show.

I charged through the horde of Padres that surrounded the San Diego pitcher and straight to the last line of defense, close enough to be able to see the terror in Show's eyes. Rick, Leon, and first base coach John Vukovich attacked from their positions as well.

Alert umpire Charlie Williams grabbed Show by the arm and raced him over to the Padre dugout. I pursued with every ounce of strength I could muster. Half a second earlier and I would have gotten him before he scampered down the dugout stairs, just ahead of my grasp.

The battle continued long after Rick and I were ejected from the game and I was rushed to Northwestern Hospital. Twenty-one-year-old pitching phenom Greg Maddux and manager Gene Michael were ejected in the fourth inning for drilling the Padre's catcher Benito Santiago. Trillo was ejected shortly after for throwing a case of sunglasses out on the field. Right-hander Scott Sanderson and interim manager Johnny Oates were the last to go, tossed out by home plate umpire Gary Darling after Sanderson threw at Padre Chris Brown in the eighth inning.

Tony Gwynn of the Padres, one of the finest hitters in the league, commented after the game, "Today was the first time in my life that I've been scared to go to the plate. I don't know how I got out of the way of some of those pitches that Sanderson threw. I'm just glad that I used to play basketball."

By 1987, I had already led the league a few times in being hit by pitches. So I understood the value of the inside pitch to the game.

I never criticized a pitcher for throwing inside. That's part of his job. But in Show's case, he wasn't just trying to brush me back. He was trying to put not only my livelihood but my life in danger.

By that time in my career, I had been hit in the head three times. The first time happened in 1982 in Los Angeles, when Bobby Castillo hit me in the face. Though I was hospitalized, the injury I sustained wasn't serious.

But the injury I sustained from Show's beaning was so severe that a plastic surgeon had to be called in. It took twenty stitches to close the wound. The surgeon did a good job of pulling the scar down into the area of my mustache so it wouldn't be so visible.

Show thought it best to write me a personal apology as a way of clearing his name. In it he went into a long-winded rendition about how he sincerely regretted hitting me with his unintended pitch and how he didn't believe that throwing at a batter was a part of the game. He even publicly apologized to the Cubs and to our fans that were there that day.

Even Bowa chimed in. "In my short time as a manager," he said, "I've never told a guy to hit anybody. I know some guys would, but Show isn't one of them. He was just pitching inside."

For days Show kept defending himself. "I can recall no other time in history where a beaning incident, an unintentional one and an accident, has caused such furor without giving me the benefit of innocence until proven guilty," he said, obviously feeling guilty. "I can stand before God and know I did not do this intentionally. On the other hand, I'm not going to keep defending myself against the witch hunt mentality that continues to perpetrate a lie against me."

No matter what he said over and over again, it seemed more than clear to me what he was trying to do with that pitch. I chose not to honor his letter with a response. I can forgive, but I find it difficult to forget.

I did not let the injury put me on the disabled list or make me miss the All-Star game, in which I was the third leading vote-getter behind Cincinnati's Eric Davis and New York Mets' Daryl

Strawberry. My '87 appearance was the first trip to the All-Star game in four years for me. Ryne Sandberg, the Cubs' second baseman and the team's up-and-coming star, was chosen to start as well. Sutcliffe, who was leading the league in wins at the time, was also there. Timmy made it too. In fact, it was Rock's two-out triple in the top of the thirteenth inning that drove in the only two runs of the game. He had been hitless in his previous six All-Star games.

By August, I was learning what it meant to play a season at Wrigley. I could feel in my own body how the large number of day games had taken its toll on Cubbie teams of the past. In our game against the Phils on August 1, it was so hot that I didn't think that I had the strength to make it past the fifth inning. But after I'd already hit two homers in the game, I had no other choice but to give another go at hitting a third. According to some of the old guys in the dugout, "You haven't done anything unless you've hit three in a game."

In my fourth trip to the plate, I barely made it out of the dugout and into the on-deck circle. How was I going to be able to muster enough strength to hit a home run? But wouldn't you know it? With the Cubbie faithful rooting me on, the ball jumped off of my bat for my third homer of the day.

Miracles do happen. The '87 season was testimony to that fact. Not only did I have the finest season of my career, but I easily outdistanced Ozzie Smith of the Cardinals as the National League's Most Valuable Player, the first time the award had ever been given to a big leaguer on a last place team.

Thank you, Lord Jesus, and thank you, Mamma.

Across town, the White Sox, who had finished the season with a 77–85 record and a fifth place finish in their division under second-year manager Jim Fregosi, were struggling too. Like us, they were rebuilding.

Their owner, Jerry Reinsdorf, an attorney/certified public accountant turned real estate magnate, who had purchased the club from legendary Bill Veeck in 1981, had hired Larry Himes to rebuild the Sox via the club's farm system.

Himes was a lifetime baseball man. A native of California, he had attended the University of Southern California, where he was an All-American selection as catcher. After graduating from USC in 1961, he went on to play in the Cincinnati Reds' farm system, where, having never reached the major leagues, he stayed until 1969. In 1970 and 1971 he coached at Mid-Pacific Institute in Honolulu and at the California Polytechnical Institute. The following year he officially began his scouting career with the Kansas City Royals.

By 1974, he had acquired a full-time scouting position with the California Angels and spent 1975 to 1978 managing the club's Idaho Falls Rookie League affiliate, where he was twice named Manager of the Year.

In 1980 Himes joined the Baltimore Orioles as their scouting supervisor and national cross-checker before returning to the Angels as their director of scouting. In 1982 he added player development responsibilities and remained with the Angels until joining the White Sox in 1986.

Himes inherited a club that had risen to prominence in 1983 under Reinsdorf and manager Tony LaRussa. However, the club had fallen fast since then. By 1984, they had dropped to fourth, and in 1985, they wound up twelve games under .500. By the following season, LaRussa had been fired and Fregosi, a take-charge guy, was brought in to run the club.

CHAPTER TWENTY-SEVEN

Our Prayers Are Answered

By the time that I had joined the Cubs, the name Dallas Green, after only five years, had become synonymous with the team. He had quickly converted the Cubs from perennial cellar dwellers to world-class champions. "No one will ever outwork us," he proclaimed at his signing. "When I hire someone, he had better work at it or hear from me."

Green immediately hired his former teammate and close friend from his days with the Phillies, Lee Elia, to manage the Cubs. He eliminated the cords of "deadwood" players and signed several top-notch replacements: catcher/first baseman/third baseman Keith Moreland, right-handed pitchers Don Larson and Dickie Noles, and Ryne Sandberg.

But by 1983, the best the club could do was a fifth-place finish. In a difficult decision, Green fired Elia and eventually replaced him with Jim Frey, who had led the Kansas City Royals to the 1980 World Series against the Phillies. In addition, Green signed two other Phillies who had played for him—Bob Dernier and "the Sarge," Gary

Matthews. With them, the club scurried away with its first division pennant in forty years. The only thing that kept them from going to the World Series was a fifth-game loss to the San Diego Padres in the National League Championship Series.

During the '85 season, the Cubbies fell to a disappointing fourth-place finish. A third of the way through 1986, nothing seemed to change; so Green was forced to fire Frey, whom he eventually replaced with Gene Michael. Having seemingly accomplished the impossible in 1984, the relationship between Green and the Tribune died a slow death. But with the costs of running a baseball team rising rapidly and the Cubs' poor finishes hurting receipts at the gate, the cost-conscious Tribune Company began reeling in Green. He finally resigned at the end of the '87 season to pursue other interests, and Frey was hired back to the team as his replacement.

Green had not left the cupboards bare for his old friend, however. Going into the '88 season, besides myself, several Cubs were coming off substantial seasons. Sutcliffe led the league with 18 wins. Big Lee Smith tossed in 36 saves. Jerry Mumphrey turned in a solid season hitting .333, and youngster Dave Martinez hit .292. As well, the Cubbie farm system, which had been supervised by Frey the previous season, was teeming with prospects.

One of the first things Frey did as general manager was to hire his close friend and one of the most respected men in the game, Don Zimmer, to manage the team. Zimmer and Frey had grown up and played ball together in Cincinnati. In fact, Western High School, where Frey pitched and played first base and Zimmer played shortstop in 1949, has produced several other grads into the big leagues, including the legendary Pete Rose. Unlike Frey, Zim had had an illustrious career as a big leaguer before turning to coaching and managing. His humble yet strong approach made him a natural as a manager.

Every bit as aggressive in the front office as his high school buddy was on the field, Frey began making every effort to keep Stan Cook, who was being nudged out of his position with the Tribune, abreast of his moves, educating him about the inner workings of the great game.

Entering 1988 the Cubs were planning on a roster resembling a tapestry of the old and the new. Out were veterans Scott Sanderson and catcher Jodie Davis. Expected to gain significant playing time were names such as first baseman Mark Grace, outfielder Rafael Palmiero, catcher Damon Berryhill, and pitcher Calvin Schrialdi. As well, many of the younger guys who recently joined the club, like pitchers Greg Maddux and Jamie Moyer and shortstop Shawon Dunston, were to be given the opportunity to lead the Cubs into the next decade.

On my end, even though baseball grossed over one billion dollars in 1987, I was left to fight it out with the Cubs for my salary in 1988. Supposedly the Cubs did not want to pay me more than Sutcliffe. I was therefore left with two choices: I could give in to their offer of 1.8 million dollars for the season, $200,000 less than what I felt I deserved. Or I could reject the Cubs' offer, go to arbitration, and have our dilemma settled legally. I chose the latter.

Arbitration is an elegant term for an ugly argument. In an attempt to justify why their claim is the correct one, each side appears before an agreed-on arbitrator, usually an attorney or a judge, and battle it out by ripping each other apart.

Our debate with the Cubs was not as ugly as I had heard some had been, though it was not pleasant either. The Cubs were adamant in comparing my statistics over the previous few years with those of players who were making the same amount, but both Dick Moss and I felt confident about our chances of winning. As we left the hearing, Dick whispered to me, "No way can the arbitrator rule against us."

But the arbitrator did rule against us. In spite of that, the Cubs, sensing a record-setting television deal with CBS on the horizon, came back two months later and offered me a two-year deal for about 6.5 million dollars. Baseball is a funny business. The Cubs had risked breaking relations with me for good by fighting over $200,000 in January, only to come back two months later and offer me even more than I would have asked for!

All things considered, life was great in Chicago. With the young guys performing far above expectations, the team took a turn for the better in 1988, finishing fourth. I finished third in the league with a .303 average, led the National League in multi-hit games, ended up second in hits and total bases, and fifth in total bases. In addition, feeling spry with all the young kids around me, I stole home for the second time in my career in a June 9 game against Pittsburgh. That same year, I became only the seventh outfielder in the history of baseball to win eight or more Golden Glove Awards. And for the first time, I began receiving the endorsements that other major leaguers, who had been playing for teams located in the United States, routinely received.

H appiness is contagious, and with everything going so well for us in Chicago, Vanessa and I again began craving the opportunity to bring a child into the world. Having tried without success the previous five years, our fears that she wouldn't be able to get pregnant began to grow. I tried to reassure my wife that we would be okay even if she never had a child.

But Vanessa is a headstrong individual, which is one of the reasons I love her so much. When she sets her mind on accomplishing something, nothing will stand in her way. That's why she was finding this whole fertility problem so difficult to deal with. She had been willing to do almost anything to rectify the situation, and we were doing everything right. We were monitoring her cycle, consistently checking her temperature. This was the only area of our life together that wasn't going the way that we wanted it to. That's probably what made it stand out so prevalently.

Though we had sought the assistance of a fertility specialist in the past, we hadn't met with success. We had tried a multitude of procedures, including artificial insemination. But that procedure didn't take, and the ovulatory-enhancing drugs Vanessa had to take drove her hormones crazy. One minute she'd get so hot so fast that she couldn't get her coat off fast enough. The very next minute she'd be freezing to death. I was beginning to wonder if, with all the frustration and aggravation, continuing to try so hard was worth it. But Vanessa was determined to leave no stone unturned to have a child, and that's just the way that it was.

By the '88 season, as we were groping for a solution, Vanessa heard some great things about Dr. LeMaire at the University of Miami's Jackson Memorial Center. In him we found a source we could believe in. He was the type of take-charge, authoritative person I like to deal with. We told him we needed something that offered the highest chance of success. And we needed it *now*, before we gave up trying to have a child and before we experienced any more unnecessary stress or expense.

LeMaire suggested that we have what he called a "mix," a less complicated procedure than in-vitro fertilization, yet as effective in most cases. With in-vitro, eggs are removed from the woman and an actual sperm is implanted inside an egg. Then the fertilized egg is embedded within the woman's uterine wall. From there it is left to grow into an embryo and eventually into a baby. A mix differs in that a woman's eggs are mixed with freshly extracted sperm from the man. Then the mixture is injected into one of the woman's fallopian tubes, where fertilization normally takes place. From there, any fertilized egg will hopefully move down the tube and into the uterus, where it needs to embed itself for an embryo to begin to grow.

Although the procedure has a success rate of only fifteen percent, one of the nice features about either the mix or the in-vitro approach is that, through the use of continual blood testing, a couple knows within four or five days whether a pregnancy has resulted. Such a quick response time is important to any couple who has been trying unsuccessfully to get pregnant.

We could hardly believe it when we got the news. Dr. LeMaire's office left a message on our answering machine that Vanessa was pregnant! Vanessa was so happy and relieved that she started to cry. We still have the tape. Even now when we play it back, it's hard to hold back tears.

On the other side of Chicago, despite drafting future American League Cy Young Award winner Jack McDowell, eventual American League Most Valuable Player Frank Thomas, and soon-to-be All-Star third baseman Robin Ventura, Himes's inability to deal humanly with people was what was making the headlines.

For example, Himes had brought along with him from Idaho Falls, where he had managed eighteen- and nineteen-year-olds, a twenty-five page book that explained his code of conduct expected of all the players and club personnel. It detailed instructions from how to dress to how to handle routine situations that big leaguers already are accustomed to dealing with. It was mandatory reading.

The White Sox general manager, à la Humphrey Bogart in the movie *The Caine Mutiny*, became obsessed with the enforcement of his petty rules and regulations. He was so obsessed with adherence to his code that it wasn't unusual for him, like a troll creeping up from beneath a bridge, to sneak up behind a player, reach under a pant leg of his trousers, and grab his ankle to verify he was indeed wearing socks.

Himes was especially tough on manager Fregosi, a world-class guy. Himes was always in his face, telling him what players he wanted in the line-up and what pitchers he wanted him to use. Himes also spent a lot more time around the clubhouse than is normal for a general manager, making everyone from the equipment guy to the players feel as if they were being spied on. Everyone on the White Sox team was getting edgy.

CHAPTER TWENTY-EIGHT

King Darius

With all the wonderful things happening to us in Chicago, by 1989 I had everything I had ever wanted from baseball. I had knowledgeable fans who adored me. I had become a local hero. I had won a long-awaited Most Valuable Player award. Vanessa had gotten pregnant. To me Chicago was the greatest town in the world, a city where dreams came true.

It was hard to believe I had been blessed with being a part of the club that Frey had put together for the '89 season. We were solid from top to bottom with young studs Mark Grace at first and Ryne Sandberg at second, hard-hitting and athletic Dunston (also an upbeat and motivating guy) at shortstop, and dependable Vance Law at third. In the outfield, I was joined by young but dependable Jerome Walton and Dwight Smith. Behind the plate, Berryhill had come into his own.

With Rick Sutcliffe, Greg Maddux, Mike Bielecki, and Scott Sanderson on the mound, we boasted of one of the top starting staffs in the game. For late-inning work out of the bullpen, we had wild and crazy, but effective, Mitch Williams.

Life was so relaxed and so good in Chicago that it was easy to be on the top of your game. No one gave you any hassles. The fans always appreciated you and came out to see you play. Frey and Zimmer had done a great job, working night and day, trying to build us into a pennant-winning team. What more could I want?

I had several great moments during the '89 season. On April 23 I hit my 300th career home run off Mets' Ron Darling. A few weeks later I tied a Cub record with eight consecutive hits from May 4–6. But my right knee was up to its old tricks again. Unable to perform, I was put on the disabled list on May 7, eventually going under the knife on May 11.

Activated June 13 and hitting .307 before the surgery, I picked up right where I had left off. For the sixth time, I was selected to the National League All-Star team. On August 18, I got my 2000th hit in Houston off Jim Clancy, proudly making me the only player in major league history besides Willie Mays to get at least 2,000 hits, 300 homers, and 300 stolen bases. So good was I feeling about the team and myself down the final stretch that I motored around the bases, achy for my second career inside-the-park-homer, which I got off Montreal's Bryn Smith on September 25.

Because of Frey's intelligent acquisitions, Zimmer's patience and guidance, especially with some of the younger players, and the maturation of the club as a whole, we improved sixteen games in the standings over the previous year, easily outdistancing the '88 champion New York Mets, who had won 100 games. Everybody seemed to come through. Maddux took over as the ace of our staff with 19 wins and a 2.95 ERA. Sutcliffe turned in 16 wins, Bielecki 18, and Sanderson 11. Williams notched 36 saves, second only to single season record-holder Mark Davis of San Diego.

On the hitting side, Grace hit .314, Ryne homered 30 times, and, despite playing only 118 games, I hit 21 homers and drove in 77 runs.

Yet the most amazing part of the season was that while Frey was in the process of building the Cubs into our division pennant winner, he also sliced the club's payroll by over thirty percent, from about 19 million dollars to 13 million.

The '89 season was a great year for Chicago Cub fans. Even though we lost four games to one to the San Francisco Giants and a red hot Wil Clark in the National League Championship Series, we had a lot to be proud of. We had proven that we were a team to be reckoned with.

The highlight of my personal life, however, came on August 12 when our son was born in Chicago. No matter how many national exposure and high pressure situations I had been in up to that time, I don't think that I was ever so nervous in my life when labor started.

By the time Vanessa and I arrived at the hospital, she was already almost fully dilated. The hospital staff took her immediately to the operating room. Though I tried to remain calm and cool, I was such a mess that I pulled on the operating room scrubs they provided over my clothes. I was sweating so much that I perspired through both layers. After our son's birth, Vanessa and I took some time before deciding to name him Darius DeAndre, after the King Darius in the Bible.

Other great things happened in 1989. In the grievance filed by the Major League Players Association, an arbitrator decided that the owners had to pay me and a group of other big leaguers, including Timmy, a combined 10.5 million dollars because of their collusion that prohibited us from getting the kind of free agency contract we deserved.

Cro turned in one of the finest seasons ever recorded by any professional athlete when he led the Japanese Baseball League in hitting, was named their MVP, and spearheaded his team to a World Series crown, where he was also named as the Most Valuable Player.

Dallas Green found himself back in the dugout with the New York Yankees, who had been looking for a fiery manager to lead them to the pennant. Unfortunately, his tenure with the team was cut short before the end of the season when he critically referred to Yankee owner George Steinbrenner as Manager George, because of his constant meddling with the line-up and rotation.

Furthermore, the owners signed a lucrative national television deal that gave each club an additional seven million dollars a year, and attendance boomed to over 50 million. On the player's end, the average big league salary had skyrocketed to $500,000 a year, and over twenty players were making two million dollars or more a year.

On the south side of Chicago with the White Sox, everything remained as topsy turvy as before. Fregosi and his team turned in another poor season. Faced with having to make a change, Reinsdorf, possibly because of his general manager's long-term deal, decided to fire Fregosi rather than Himes. Jeff Torborg, who had been around professional baseball the last quarter of a century, was named as their new manager. Besides managing the Indians between 1977 and 1979, Torborg also had several other claims to fame. He had been the catcher for Sandy Koufax's perfect game in 1965, Bill Singer's no-hitter in 1970, and the fifth of Don Drysdale's record six consecutive shutouts.

But in Chicago Jeff ran into more than he could handle. With Fergosi out of the way, Himes possessed the control over a big league team that he had always sought. In fact, when he traded Harold Baines, the Sox's most popular player, to Texas for future star Wilson Alvarez, eventual All-Star Sammy Sosa, and infielder Scott Fletcher, he didn't even inform Reinsdorf or Torborg, both of whom embarrassingly had to learn about it from outside sources.

Still, even with all the grief that Himes deservedly received from Reinsdorf and Torborg and from the media, he continued to check for bare ankles on the players!

CHAPTER TWENTY-NINE

The Miracle Child

Between the '89 and '90 seasons, just when life was going great and we felt we had it all, tragedy seemed to be lurking at our doorstep. Vanessa became quite ill. Fearing it was something serious based on all the gynecological problems she had a history of having, she delayed going to the doctor for almost two months.

Finally we had to make an appointment. Our doctor ran all the usual tests and was able to make a quick and shocking diagnosis. She was pregnant again! Neither of us could believe it. The fatigue and nausea were simply signs that she was with child. Words cannot describe how happy we were, especially after all the trouble we had trying to have Darius. I'll never forget Vanessa telling me, "I bought one child and now I'm getting one for free." Then she'd chuckle, unable to believe our good fortune herself.

With my new family, winning baseball games wasn't nearly as important to me as it once had been. That, of course, did not mean that I gave it less effort in my playing. In reality, it meant that I was able to give it more because I was putting less pressure on myself.

Entering the '90 season, I wanted to secure a contract for the following year before that season began. By the time we struck a deal for 1991 with an option for 1992 around mid-season, I was well on the way to one of the finest seasons in my career. I had already been named as the National League Player of the Month for May by hitting .350 with 9 homers and 28 RBI, and I had landed a place on the All-Star team for the seventh time, my sixth as a starter.

Amber Chanelle was born on September 5. Even though we were out of the pennant race by then, life was still looking good. I wound up hitting a career high .310 batting average, finished ninth in the National League with 27 homers, sixth with 100 RBIs, fifth in slugging percentage with a .535 average, and tenth in extra base hits. I was also tied for the most intentional walks, including a big league record five in one game versus Cincinnati on May 22.

Maddog Maddux turned in another sterling year with a 15–5 record, as did Ryno with a .306 average, 40 home runs, and 100 RBIs, and Mark Grace, who hit .309 with 82 RBIs.

It was our pitching that fell apart for us in 1990, probably the single most important reason why we weren't competitive enough to defend our championship. Besides Maddog and rookie Mike Harkey, who turned in a 12–6 season, we didn't have much. Bielecki's record fell to 8–11 while his ERA zoomed to 4.93, and Sutcliffe sustained an injury early in the season that knocked him out for the remainder of the year. In the bullpen, newcomer Paul Assenmacher and Williams together were able to combine for only 26 saves, ten less than Mitch had produced by himself the year before.

Even though we dropped sixteen games in the standings and finished three spots behind the first-place Pirates, not winning the pennant again in 1990 had nothing to do with lack of effort or mistakes on the part of Frey or Zimmer. What happened to our pitching staff simply happens in the game of baseball.

On the national front, good things were also happening with the owners, who signed a record four-year 1.45 billion dollar deal with CBS. As a result, not only did the value of local TV deals skyrocket but the worth of actual franchises as well.

In the front office, an aging and reluctant Stan Cook was gradually being pushed into retirement by the Tribune Company. To pacify him into accepting the move, the Tribune appointed him as the Cubs' Chairman of the Board.

During the '90 season, Himes was still making a laughingstock of himself at Comisky Park. The final straw between him and the White Sox came when he, thoroughly possessive of the ball club, actually chased owner Reinsdorf off his own field before a group of well-informed witnesses, screaming at his boss to "Leave my team alone!"

No matter how good an eye for talent Himes had, no matter that the Sox were making a run at the pennant, no matter how many years Reinsdorf was obligated to pay him for, the White Sox general manager was fired. Considering all that the players, Reinsdorf, and the two managers who had worked under Himes had tolerated, no one was terribly surprised at his being relieved.

Shortly thereafter, with Frey and Zim's jobs in jeopardy because of the Cubs' poor season in 1990, it seems that Stan Cook began to receive detailed evaluations from an obviously knowledgeable source, second-guessing everything his general manager and manager were doing with the Cubs. Each evaluation was supposedly efficiently and professionally arranged. The preparer also apparently began to telephone Cook on a regular basis, offering verbal comments and criticisms.

Although none of this was public information at the time, it seemed as if someone was after the jobs of Frey and Zimmer.

CHAPTER THIRTY

Changes Again

Most of my teammates and I realized that Zim and Frey were both on the hot seat entering the '91 season, but we were not aware of what was going on in the front office that would eventually affect them directly. In fact, I doubt if either Frey or Zim felt anything unusual going on. From our team's standpoint, they were doing their best to put a winning ball club on the field.

One of our goals that season was to save Frey and Zim's jobs by bringing another pennant back to the Windy city. To enhance our chances, Frey had gotten several impact players during the off-season. He added all-time Toronto Blue Jay home run hitter George Bell to play left field, Houston Astro all-time save leader Dave Smith to replace Williams (whom he had traded to Philadelphia), and Danny Jackson, a left-handed starter who, as a Cincinnati Red in 1988, had led the National League in wins with twenty-three.

However, only thirty-seven games into the season, we didn't look much better than the previous season. A scapegoat had to be found, and Zim was the logical choice. Almost overnight, he went from being regarded as the finest field general in the game in 1989, when he was named as the Manager of the Year by the Baseball Writers' Association of America, *The Sporting News,* and United Press International, to being unemployed. In the high-exposure national market of Chicago and with the Cubs boasting one of the highest payrolls in the game, Frey was forced to fire Zim to keep his own job.

Jim Essian, who had been a strong-armed journeyman catcher for the White Sox, Phillies, Athletics, Mariners, and Indians, and who was one of the least confrontational men you will ever meet, was hired to take over on a temporary basis.

When Essian worked as manager in the minor leagues, he routinely protected his players by arguing a call with an umpire at the drop of a hat. But once he was elevated to his post with the Cubs, all of that changed. He never protected his players either from the umpires or from the ploys of the opposing team. We really missed Zim. Finishing the season with a 59-63 record, it was obvious to everyone that not only Essian would be gone but Frey as well.

By the time Cook fired Frey as the Cubs' general manager, he didn't have to call any other teams for recommendations on whom to hire. The Chairman of the Cubs knew the person he wanted, the same man who was rumored to have been sending him the well-organized and efficient evaluations for the last year or so—Larry Himes. Supposedly, Cook didn't even call the White Sox to check out Himes's background. Apparently thrilled with the possibility of making a success out of an executive who had been let go by his club's cross-town rival, Cook had already been sold.

The White Sox owner, Reinsdorf, who would now be relieved of the money he still owed Himes for the final year on his contract, issued a smiley-faced press release through his media relations department: "We are happy for the White Sox and pleased for the Cubs."

CHAPTER THIRTY-ONE

A Year Enduring the Dark Side

As I entered the '92 season, security, not money, was my primary concern. I wanted to play two more seasons and then retire at the age of forty as a Chicago Cub. Based on my accomplishments with the Cubs since 1987 and my performance over the last few seasons, averaging 28 homers and 102 RBIs, I didn't think a two-year agreement was asking too much.

When Dick Moss approached Himes in the off-season about negotiating a new contract, the general manager put him off time and time again, though we were not concerned about being able to work something out. That changed, however, when the club began making a concerted effort to sign free agent Bobby Bonilla, formerly of the Pittsburgh Pirates and a natural right fielder, to a record 23 million dollar, five-year contract. Until then, I had never questioned my position as the club's right fielder.

Based on what the Cubs were trying to do with Bonilla, who eventually signed with the Mets, we felt it was best to reapproach Himes to see if he was even interested in extending my career with the

Cubs. Again, he verified that he was indeed interested but that he was too busy at the present time.

Himes put us off for five months until he finally bowed to the pressure of the media and fans by offering me a $300,000 pay cut, with a club option at the same rate for the following year. I thought he was kidding. But Himes proved how serious he was when he set a deadline for me to accept or reject his offer. There would be no negotiations.

I couldn't believe how I was being treated. All of the free agents that the Cubs had signed the previous few years, sight unseen, had been given far more respect that I was being offered. Yet Himes approached us as if I was fortunate to be offered anything at all. After careful reflection, I concluded that if I was going to have to take a pay cut after all I had accomplished and was still capable of doing, I would retire before doing so.

After Himes's deadline passed, he let it be known through his negotiator, Dennis Homerin, that the Cubs had been unable to meet my wishes of having contract negotiations concluded before the end of spring training. That announcement made me look like the bad guy. He went on to tell the press that he would not be able to consider negotiating a new contract with me until after the upcoming expansion draft. The Cubs, he said, didn't want to be forced to use up one of the valuable spaces reserved to protect younger players and veterans in the prime of their careers. All of that made sense to me. So Dick requested that we try to reach an agreement after the expansion draft. Himes declined.

It was becoming apparent to me that Himes's reasons for denying any negotiations went far beyond his consideration for me as a player. I was too strong a person to his liking. An anecdote that Billy Connors told me during spring training about Himes put it in a nutshell. Billy, who had worked miracles as Zim's pitching coach in 1989 and was one of the most respected mentors in the game, told me that Himes had scolded him once for highlighting a few details in one of his scouting reports in red ink.

"'Don't ever write in red ink again,'" Billy said Himes told him. "'Only I write in red.'"

It was obvious after spending a few weeks working under him that the other coaches had lost a lot of respect for Himes. A coach's life was frustrating under him. After a long day, when most of them had shown up early in the morning and were looking forward to going home and relaxing for the evening, Himes, whose work day supposedly started around their quitting time, often called a meeting and spent most of the time going over goal-setting, a topic with which he was obsessed. Rarely did he want to discuss how the Cubs were going to win ball games.

Frank Howard, who has been around baseball for over three decades, first as a player and then as a coach and manager, summarized it best when he said in reference to Himes, "When you apply a minor league mentality to the major leagues, you get three things: loss of confidence, lack of communication, and total chaos."

At least after frequent meetings on the setting of goals, the coaches were able to wring some incentive bonuses out of Himes. If Connors, for example, consistently met his goals, the general manager promised him a $10,000 bonus at the end of the season.

Shortly after Dick's last attempt to get Himes to speak to us in the spring, I had my first personal confrontation with him. During the off-season or when I'm lounging around home with my family, you can usually find me in a T-shirt with a pair of jeans, shorts, or sweats. But during the season, when I'm officially a member of a major league baseball team, I take a pride in how I look and dress.

Going into the '92 season, I had a tailor personally design some lapelless jackets for me, which I could wear with turtleneck sweaters during the cold first few weeks of the season. These jackets cost about $700 apiece. Since they were lapelless, I couldn't wear a necktie, thus violating one of the rules in Himes's code of conduct book, which he had brought over with him from the White Sox. I just about went wild when Himes tried to reprimand me for not wearing a tie, especially when others on the club were mocking the entire situation by wearing jeans, cowboy boots, and flannel shirts, on top of which they placed scraggly old ties.

I didn't want to confront Himes directly, for it would not have been proper to go over our manager's head. So I talked to our new manager, Jim Lefebvre. Though his position with the Cubs constituted only his second big league managing job and it was rumored that he had only been hired by Himes because he would be easy to control, this former switch-hitting Dodger infielder had been around the game much longer than Larry. Even though out of respect for his boss he couldn't let on to me how ridiculous he felt the situation was, he promised to take the issue up with Himes. True to his word, a few days later he got back to me and explained that he had worked everything out and that it was okay for me to wear the jackets.

It was right after that episode that Himes stopped talking to me for good. Not that he had been vocal with me up to that time, but at least he had occasionally acknowledged my presence. He refused even to look at me whenever he walked past me. In fact, one time he entered the clubhouse with Barry Rozner, a reporter with the *Daily Herald* whom he wasn't particularly fond of, and me there. Faced with the decision of speaking either to me or to Rozner, Himes chose the latter.

The situation became so absurd that even my teammates began to notice how Himes ignored my presence. They kept making jokes about it, and I laughed along with them. But I admit that I was falling apart inside. It wasn't that I cared so much about how Himes felt about me. I just wasn't used to being hated.

By the second week of the season, Himes's controlling ways took hold of us. The effect had filtered down through Lefebvre and the coaches to the players. I can't speak for the others, but I began to feel as if I was constantly being watched or spied upon and that every move I made was the wrong one.

On my end, the love that I felt for the game was giving way to frustration, and I was contemplating walking away from the game right then and there. My left knee, the one that I had hurt playing football, was in need of being cleaned out again and the bone spurs on the joint shaved down. The strength I usually possessed to endure the pain wasn't there. Surgery seemed like a welcome alternative to putting up with this mess. Though I was leading the team in RBIs and tied for the team lead in home runs, I dreamed of artificial knee joints and the surgery that would end the pain, and my career, for good. Even Dr. Schafer, the club's orthopedic surgeon, remarked that my knees were worse than Chicago Bear Dan Hampton's, worse than Dick Butkus's, and probably worse than anyone else's in professional sports. He stated I had the highest threshold for pain that he had ever run across, and he seconded my recommendation for replacement surgery later in life.

It's amazing what a man like Himes can do to your soul. Mamma had told me about devils and how to handle them, but she had never schooled me about anyone like Himes.

Fight as I did, everything that he was trying to do to me finally got to me. By August I couldn't take the tension and uncertainty anymore, and I fell into a 12-for–86 slump. My mind was no longer in the game. Despite my 13 homers and 51 runs during the first half of the season, suddenly all those who had been on my bandwagon jumped off, all but Lefebvre. Risking his job, he stuck his neck out for me. While others were calling for my retirement, he publicly defended me. "He's still got a lot left," he clearly stated. "I guarantee it."

His comment was like a voice from heaven. That little bit of reassurance was all I needed to get me out of the doldrums. Just a hand to help pull me off the mat was enough. I became determined not to let Himes destroy me. From that point on, I showed my worth by going on a five-week rampage to end the season. All of my advocates returned, stopped griping about my knees, and began talking about my heart again.

While all of this was going on, Himes was doing his best to come between myself and the Cubs. He called for a meeting with Lefebvre and the coaches on a road trip into

Philadelphia to discuss the upcoming season. When the topic of potential right fielders came up, he went down the list of free agents who would be available—especially Rubin Sierra in Texas, whom he really liked—and the players whom he felt he could land in a trade.

The coaches couldn't believe what they were hearing. "Our club has the best all-around right fielder in the league over the last ten years, so why aren't they interested in re-signing him?" asked coach Chuck Cottier. A few others joined in as well. But Himes refused to give any credence to their inquiries and continued with his next topic.

Jose Martinez, realizing the difficulty of my position, cautioned me after the meeting, "They have enough money to sign you. But you will have to make it clear that you want to stay with the Cubs, and then do your best not to do anything to embarrass Himes through the media."

The coaches were also supportive of me. In fact, Tom Treblehorn was the only one who didn't push Himes for a long-term arrangement with me, though he did feel that I should at least be offered contract laden with incentive bonuses.

With three days left in the season, the team having been out of the pennant race for a few months and everybody counting down the hours until we could go home, I limped out of the training room after undergoing an icing of my knees, the first part of my daily physical therapy routine. All the players were waiting for me. Everyone was silent.

It was obvious that they were looking for me to say something. I realized what they wanted, a christening to the end of a miserable year in Chicago, so I gave it to them.

Smiling slightly as I looked everyone in the eye, I threw the towels I had been holding into my locker. "That's it," I said. "Let's go home. It's time to go home."

The final day of the season was special for me. During the chapel service that morning, everyone in attendance was given an opportunity to give a testimony or to say a few words about the season.

Realizing that 1992 might be my last season in Chicago, I thanked all my teammates for their support and friendship during my tenure with the Cubs. Unsure whether I would see them anymore on a regular basis, I encouraged them to continue to work hard and to get the most out of their time in the majors.

I also thanked Ned Colletti, the club's assistant general manager, for all that he had done for me and for being the special friend that he was. I concluded by reminding them not to allow the continual trials and tribulations that life was sure to provide to sway them away from their love and respect for the Lord.

Later that day, I stepped up to the plate for my final at-bat of the season in Wrigley Field. The 23,000 loyal Cub fans rose to their feet to cheer me on. The pitcher went to a 3–2 count on me. There was no way that he was going to give me anything to hit in that situation, especially after I had hit my 399th home run earlier that day. But there was also no way that I wasn't going to swing at his next pitch.

He threw me a pitch nearly over my head and way outside. I swung anyway and struck out.

PART FIVE

Off to Boston

CHAPTER THIRTY-TWO

A Decision
I Didn't Want to Make

I wasn't the only big-name Cubbie potentially becoming a free agent after the '92 season. Maddux (aka Maddog), whom most thought to be the finest pitcher in the league, and Ryno also entered the season with the same dilemma. All of us wanted to remain Cubs, but only Ryno, who Himes felt was the class of the Cubbies, was signed. In fact, his deal, a record-breaking, five-year contract for seven and a half million dollars a season sent shock waves throughout all of professional sports. Shortly after, big league owners were all over the Tribune Company for signing Sandberg for such an astronomical amount. They were frightened that they would be expected to match that amount down the road with some of their superstars.

To lose Maddog and me without a fight would have been so detrimental for Himes that the Cubbie fans would be calling for his head. But the truth of the matter was that Maddux and I weren't his type of players. Sandberg is more soft-spoken, more of a Himes-type guy. At that stage of his career, Ryno wouldn't openly challenge Himes's sense of control.

Maddog and I were different. Though I'm far from being considered a vocal person, I do let it be known how I feel, and Maddux does the same. He'll speak out if he thinks something is wrong. Himes dislikes anyone who challenges rather than applauds him.

Throughout the course of the season, Himes made no secret of his excuse that he had to wait until after the expansion draft even to talk to me about negotiating a new contract. Taking him at his word, since the situation didn't allow us any other alternatives, my agent and I waited patiently. But the fans and media weren't as patient. Whether I would be re-signed or not was a hot topic.

On November 1, a story surfaced, quoting reliable but unnamed sources, that a deal between the Cubs and me was nearly completed and that I could be signed as early as within ten days. The deal, they were saying, would keep me in a Cub uniform for not only the next two years, but in the broadcast booth, in a coach's uniform, or maybe even as a player (if I choose to extend my playing career) for several years beyond that. It was rumored that I would be paid four million dollars over the course of the first two seasons and another one million to be split over the following eight years.

When the story came out, the media contacted me, and I called Dick, who got in touch with Homerin about the rumor. None of us knew anything about such a pact, which Himes himself may have leaked to the press to take the heat off. The truth was that we and the Cubs were light years apart from landing a deal. Based on the present market value, Dick was looking for somewhere between eleven and twelve million dollars over two years. The Cubs, who had refused to negotiate with us since the debacle at the end of spring training, had given firm indication that they could get me for far less.

Four days later I did the expected and filed for free agency, three days ahead of the major league imposed deadline. Fanning the fervor of the fans, the media took an optimistic perspective on my filing, saying that it would actually give me a better chance of remaining a Cub because the club would not have to include me on their protected list for the expansion draft.

Had we not filed, the Cubs would have been put in a difficult position by being left with two controversial alternatives. They would have had to either include me on their protected list or release me. If they had chosen the latter, they would not have been permitted to negotiate with me before May 15, 1993, by which time I would certainly have linked up with another team.

By the time the long-awaited expansion draft was over, Himes had done a lot more to make the Cubs into his type of team by acquiring Sammy Sosa from the White Sox. He also had reneged on his promise of a bonus for Connors, who was responsible for Maddux's winning the 1992 Cy Young Award and who had more than met his lofty goals. The move forced Connors to quit, which was probably part of Himes's plan all along.

According to the media's reports throughout the year, supposedly the Cubs wanted me. But Himes didn't do much to show me. The offer that he finally flung in my direction was the same one he had reluctantly made in spring training. When I didn't bite, the fans reacted, and he sweetened the pot a bit, still leaving the deal far from what I would be able to get on the open market. Himes declared that to be the club's final offer and immediately gave us a deadline. We felt that the numbers he was throwing at us were only for the media. He knew we would never accept them, but he didn't want to come off looking like a bad guy by not trying to sign me.

Thus Himes forced me into making one of the most difficult decisions of my life. The day after Dick informed him that we would not be accepting his offer, Himes held a press conference to inform the press that I had turned down the club's final offer and that I would no longer be a Chicago Cub.

As I have experienced so many times in my life, where the Lord closes a door, He always opens a window. The evening after Himes's press conference, Dick called to let me know that the Red Sox had contacted him and were interested in working out a deal. By the next morning, a contract had been worked out. I was to receive nine million dollars to be spread equally over the next two years. That offer constituted the first time in my big league career that a club had actually come after me!

Shortly after I left the Cubs, Maddux was forced out of a Cubbie uniform too, but not without a fight. Even though he eventually signed with Atlanta for five million dollars a year, leaving Chicago was the last thing he had wanted to do. In fact, according to Connors, Maddux had called the pitching coach and asked him to contact Himes for him, expressing that he was willing to take much less money than Atlanta was offering in order to stay in Chicago.

But Himes backed off from signing the Cy Young Award Winner, the kind of pitcher that you can build your entire staff around, a potential Hall of Famer. He had already acquired the services of a few free-agent hurlers, all of whom combined didn't have the ability to do for a pitching staff what Maddux's presence did.

Back in Chicago, the Tribune Company had finally been able to supposedly force Stan Cook to step down as their chairman. Cook's demotion was a move of major proportions. For years he had been one of the most powerful men in the history of the newspaper business.

As a native of Chicago who had graduated from the city's prestigious Northwestern University, Cook, the ultimate overachiever, left Shell Oil Company in 1951 to join the Tribune Company. There his natural drive and easy manner propelled him rapidly up the corporate ladder. By 1973, he had worked his way to the rank of publisher of the *Chicago Tribune*. The following year he was elected President and Chief Executive of the entire Tribune Company. From that time forward, he became the primary driving force behind making the Tribune Company the major media conglomerate that it became. It was Cook who engineered the acquisition of the Cubs from the Wrigleys for twenty million dollars, paltry by today's standards. He was also responsible for luring Dallas Green away from the Phillies and bringing baseball's most sought-after executive to the Cubs.

So Cook's apparently being forced to step down represented a major shift in the hierarchy of the Tribune. But the hard-fighting Cook was not going to slip away quietly into the night. He fought with every ounce of his energy to retain the power he had spent his lifetime achieving.

The Cubs became Cook's lone and final stronghold. Thus there was no way that he was going to fire Himes as the team's general manager, no matter how poorly he might perform. To do so would mean opening up a crease in his own armor. As a result, the Cubs found themselves stuck with the incompetent general manager at the helm. Cook could not fire him without potentially opening himself up to the same fate as well.

I admit that, even with all the money Boston was paying me, entering spring training in 1993 left me distraught over having to leave the Cubs. As time wore on, however, I got to know the guys on the club and began getting excited about playing in Boston, my first year in the American League. Within a few weeks with the club, I was able to put the past behind me.

The big concern of the Red Sox entering the '93 season was whether they were going to be able to shake the last-place finish of the previous season. That was one of the reasons why they had signed me and a couple other free agents. The front office was hoping that our presence would pull the different facets of the club back together and take it to a new level.

The rejuvenated chemistry that the club had sought seemed to work. We were hitting on all cylinders coming out of spring training. In the first twelve games of the season I hit .311 with one homer, the 400th of my career, and had 9 RBIs. We started off fast, only to hit a dry spell after the first month.

Unfortunately, early in the season, I also hurt my knee. Though I kept trying to play on it, the injury got worse. With my knee becoming a continual problem defensively in the outfield, for the first time in my career I got to taste the illusive pleasures of being a designated hitter. Though I didn't like the idea of being a DH at first, having prided myself on being an all-around player for so long, after I got used to it I liked it.

"Hey, old goat," our manager Butch Hobson had told me, however, "don't get used to DHing. I'm planning on putting you back out in right field just as soon as you're ready."

With my knee not responding to treatment, I had no alternative but to submit to surgery in early May.

Hobson still had me in the DH spot when I returned from the disabled list, but I had rushed back too quickly. My knee began stiffening up on a regular basis. Not only did I have to ice it down continually, but I also had to have it drained routinely.

When I rejoined the team in late May, they were on a hot streak, winning 23 of 29 games to pick up a dozen games in the standings and move into first place.

I DHed exclusively until the third week of July, when, feeling much better, I made a few starts in right field. Not wanting to lose my timely hitting and hot bat in the line-up, Butch didn't give me another start in the outfield until back-to-back games in Detroit on August 7 and 8.

Though we were still in the pennant race going into the last month of the season, we fell out of the running when we lost some of our big guns to injuries. For myself, on September 7 in Chicago, the White Sox's Tim Belcher broke a bone in my wrist on one of my career high thirteen hit-by-pitches. I could no longer play in the field or even grip a bat. But because of September roster action, they chose not to put me on the disabled list.

Though our young first baseman Mo Vaughn, an enthusiastic and good-natured kid, led the team in about every offensive category, I still managed to chip in with plenty of timely hitting during the '93 season. Not only did my 16 game-winning RBIs lead the club, but I also finished second on the club with 27 game-tying or go-ahead RBIs. In addition, seven of my home runs put us ahead and one homer tied the score for us.

Besides our falling out of the pennant race, the only other downside of 1993 was that I was able to play in only 121 games because of my injuries. This held me down to 13 home runs for the season, less than Timmy was able to hit with the White Sox—a fact he would make clear to me over and over again during the off-season.

CHAPTER THIRTY-THREE

Teaching—and Being Taught

During the off-season I usually take time to heal and to catch up on everything with my family. I also use the opportunity to recollect and ponder the past and the future.

Between the 1993 and 1994 seasons, I took Darius and Amber over to the cemetery where the graves of Mamma and Bo lie side by side. By then, both of my children had begun to resemble me in their own ways—especially Darius, who, even at his young age, was obsessed with the game of baseball. Each time I watch him swing a bat, I can't help feel a tickle in my heart. How wonderful it is that the Lord blesses each of us with a dream, a purpose. I only pray that I can be as faithful a channel for His love as my family was for me.

The trip to the cemetery was the first with my children. Neither of them knew either Mamma or Bo. How I wished they had!

As I stood above their gravestones, I begin to wonder why the Lord had taken these two people, both so precious in my life, before they had the opportunity to meet them. With the tiny hands of both my children in mine, the words of one of Mamma's favorite lessons came back to me again.

"Pudgy," I heard her say, "everything happens for a reason. Any time you begin to lose faith, just remember that God has a purpose for everything. Like Christ said in Matthew 10:30, 'Even the hairs of your head are numbered.'"

I thought of Bo's death. I saw where it had taught me to let go. I thought of the death of my father's mother, which had allowed me to put my relationship with his family in proper perspective. I thought of Mamma's passing, which had made me into a true believer in life after death.

Then I thought about my father-in-law, who had been an influential man in my life too. Each year before I took off for spring training, I made a special trip to see him and my mother-in-law. He always took the time to have a talk with me. Some years he repeated what he had said the year before. Other times he hit me with something totally unexpected. But either way, each one of these talks constituted a special moment for me. And each time he spoke with me, he said something I needed to hear.

I bowed my head as I thought about him. It had only been a few months before that my sister had called us. We had just gotten home after visiting my mother. I answered the phone.

"You've got to get to South Miami," she reported, obviously shaken. "Mr. Mose is on the floor and we can't wake him."

By the time we pulled up outside their home, the paramedics were working on him with the electric paddles, but he was already dead. After about fifteen minutes of trying to resuscitate him, they lifted him onto a stretcher, wheeled him outside, and took him away in an ambulance.

Though Vanessa and I felt that both Darius and Amber were too young to attend the funeral, that didn't keep him from asking us question after question about his grandfather.

"Where is granddad?" he asked. "When is he coming home?"

Initially we hoped that he would stop asking questions. But he didn't. So Vanessa and I decided to tell Darius that his granddad had died. That, of course, wasn't enough of an explanation for him.

"Why isn't he coming back?" he asked.

"Because he's up in heaven with God," I replied.

"What's heaven?" he continued.

"It's where God lives," Vanessa answered.

"You mean granddad is in heaven?"

"Yes," I said.

"Where's heaven?" was the next question. "And what's dying?"

"Heaven's up there," Vanessa answered, pointing to the sky as a plane passed overhead.

We had hoped that our discussion with Darius satisfied his curiosity about his granddad's disappearance. But as we were about to find out, it only sparked further confusion.

"Darius, what's wrong?" I asked as I drove down the road with him a few days later. He was looking up in the sky and beginning to cry. When he didn't reply, I repeated my question.

"It's granddad," he replied. "I don't want him to fall out of the plane."

"The plane?" I asked, realizing that he must have thought that Vanessa was pointing to the plane the other day when she was trying to tell Darius where heaven was located.

Answering my son's questions as best I could only led to further questions. It became obvious to me that his grandfather's death had for the first time caused him to wonder about God. As I thought about that, I again recollected what Mamma had told me over and over again, "Everything happens for a purpose."

As I now stood there in the cemetery, hand in hand with my dear children, I smiled, recalling how my father-in-law's death had opened up a whole new vein of communication between my son and me.

"What are you smiling at, Daddy?" he asked me.

"I'm just happy to be here with both of you," I said, looking down at both of them.

"Do you know what these are?" I went on to ask, pointing to the headstones as I bent down to hold them.

Both shook their heads.

"These are the headstones for your great-grandmother and your grand-uncle Theodore. They were very special people. Though they never met you, they would be very proud of me for having the two of you, more proud than for any game I ever played in or for any home run I ever hit."

"Really?" asked Darius, whose major pastime had become watching over and over again a video of me that was put together after my MVP year in Chicago, entitled *He's A Hero*.

"Really," I replied.

Three months later, as I sat on our bench before one of our games, I thought about that day. I thought about what Mamma had told me, what I had told my children, and what I felt about playing for the Red Sox.

Sure, I had been disappointed at having been forced out of Chicago. But with the Lord Jesus guiding me, more grand and glorious things had happened that I could have ever imagined.

Take, for example, my relationship with the Red Sox. I hadn't wanted to play there or to leave the Cubs—or to leave the National League, for that matter. But the Lord gave me no other alternative. Either I could leave or I could give in to everything that I didn't believe in. But looking back, I realize that if the Lord had not given me the way out of Chicago, there is no way that I would have found the beauty and pleasure that awaited me in Boston.

As a Red Sox, I have been given the room I've needed to be the leader I always wanted to be. In fact, so well has my reputation as a wise old sage become known that last year's number one draft pick, Alex Rodriguez, sought me out at one of the local public batting cages, where I regularly run into fans.

Even though we live only a five-minute drive away from each other, this was the first time we had met. He surprised me by being so down to earth for an eighteen-year-old. Having just received a record-breaking signing bonus from the Seattle Mariners, I had expected a cocky kid with a big ego.

"I'm feeling a lot of pressure," he confessed, getting right to the point. "I mean, they're expecting me to make it to the majors so fast."

"The Mariners gave you all that money for a reason," I counseled. "You have a gift. They'll take care of you. Don't put any unnecessary pressure on yourself. All you have to do is go out and play your hardest. They're going to bring you through the system. Don't worry about how quickly you get to the big leagues. They won't bring you up before your time. They have too much invested in you. You don't have to prove anything. Just continue to work hard."

He was also having problems with some of his teammates, who appeared to shun him.

"They're not intimidated by you," I told him. "They just don't know how to approach you. Believe in your abilities and realize that what's happened has happened for a reason. A lot of little things have gotten you to where you are now."

Looking back at that conversation, I realize that what I told Alex is true of all of us, including myself. In a flash, I sensed all that had helped get me to Boston, and I realized how truly fortunate I was to be there.

CHAPTER THIRTY-FOUR

A Whole New Future

No longer playing right field, I entered the '94 season with my knees feeling the best they had felt in years. Hobson knew I was feeling good and began giving me the steal sign each time I reached base. Just like the old days with the Expos—I was feeling young and spry. As a result, I strongly leaned toward playing at least another year, if not two. I felt that 3,000 hits and 500 home runs were definitely within my reach.

Then, in early May, while taking on the revitalized Cleveland Indians at Fenway Park, I hit a sharp grounder to third base and took off for first, trying to beat it out for a hit. About three-fourths of the way down the baseline, my entire left leg grabbed and became stiff. I pulled up lame as I crossed the bag, hobbled back over in the direction of my teammates, and eased myself down onto the top step of the dugout.

I sat there in pain for a few minutes, intending soon to make my way over to our trainer. However, when I tried to get up, the leg stiffened even more. Each time I put weight on it, sharp pains shot up the leg and throughout my entire body. When I finally reached the trainer, I asked him to call the team doctor. Dr. Pappas, an international authority on sports-related injuries, gave my knee a thorough examination but said little. He chose to reserve his evaluation of my condition until the following morning.

I didn't have to call him the next morning. He was on the phone to me bright and early. He had a good idea that I wouldn't be feeling any better. He recommended I go under the knife. That way he could repair the torn cartiledge that I had suffered in the knee. Two days later I was wheeled into surgery.

I wanted desperately to start playing again as soon as possible. Within two weeks, I was in my regular spot in the line-up.

Though I experienced some discomfort as I jogged before each game, I found that I could usually massage out the tension and release the pressure I was feeling around the knee. But that didn't last. Before long, I found it nearly impossible to run. However, since there was no swelling around the knee, I decided to hang in there.

With the Red Sox doing so well, I didn't want to quit my role as designated hitter. But with my knee acting up, it was becoming more and more of a realistic possibility that I might have to stick with my original plan of playing until I was forty, in which case the '94 season would be my last. If that's the way it had to be, in no way did I want to go out limping and grimacing. Like most big leaguers, I wanted to go out on a bang with a career year or a championship ring, or both. So I kept forcing my body back out onto the field each day.

Then, on my fortieth birthday, as if the Lord was trying to send me a message, my knee locked up again. This time it was worse. Our trainer gave me a shot of cortizone in the knee and told me to take a few days off.

After coming back, I felt gimpy and weak-legged. It locked up again during our final July game against the A's in Oakland. In Anaheim, the next stop on our West Coast swing, I asked for and got another cortizone shot—my second in less than ten days.

While there, I decided to have the knee checked out by a Dr. Yocum, who gave me a thorough examination, complete with X-rays. Then he sat down to share with me what I had already been sensing. My time was up. With my knees as bad as they were, playing was no longer an option, unless I wanted to severely risk the quality of my post-baseball life. The fact that I would someday have to have the joints in both knees surgically replaced had long been a given. However, according to Yocum, if I kept playing, I would need to have the replacements done much earlier than I had planned.

When we returned from the West Coast, even without any physical pressure applied to it, my knee locked up on me again—this time in the middle of the night. Once again I called Pappas. He had one of his associates check it out in the morning, thinking I may have contracted an infection from one of the cortizone shots. Though no trace of an infection was found, I was put on the DL for the second time that season. This gave me an opportunity to take a good, hard look at my life.

I have been blessed with a lot of attributes, one of which is my ability to concentrate on a goal and then go out and get it. But there is a bad side to this character trait. Though my ability to focus with such intensity had driven me through years of pain with my knees, it was now robbing me of a greater understanding. It took the incredibly severe pain I had been experiencing during previous few months to reflect on various aspects of my life.

Like every kid who has ever dreamt of being a big leaguer, I wanted play on a World Series winning team. Naturally, I wanted my final season to end with a bang. However, in my own selfish way, I had forgotten how truly blessed I had been in my career. The Lord had carried me through, over, and around one trying experience after another. He had made me a hero in the eyes of baseball fans everywhere, and most importantly, in the eyes of my son. He had answered each one of my prayers. He had given me the opportunity to play until my fortieth birthday, which had been a goal of mine ever since I had made it to the big leagues.

But I had gotten greedy. Because the Lord had blessed me with good physical health at the beginning of the '94 season, I started dreaming of the World Series ring, the 3,000 hits, and the 500 home runs, instead of being thankful for the opportunity to conclude my career by ending it on a high note. The pain in my knee was all I needed to remind me of where I had strayed. It was the Lord's way of jolting me back to reality.

Consequently, I am no longer measuring myself against the material. I am thankful for the blessings I have received from the Lord. I can live with myself. I can walk away from the game in a joyful remembrance of all the love the Lord has bestowed on me throughout this phase of my life. I can also walk away knowing that the Lord has something planned for me beyond the game. What is that? I don't know. However, I know it must be important in the scheme of his world. Why else would He be so adamant about my making a transition out of baseball? Whatever it is, I'll know it when it comes. I'll know it because I'll be listening and because He'll show it to me over and over again.

My advice to any of you who read this book is to go when the Lord calls, wherever and whenever He calls. Go whether you understand why He is calling or not. Just go. For each one of us is important to Him, and each one of us has a purpose that only He knows.

He loves us with a love beyond our comprehension, and He leads us for reasons that may lie beyond our understanding. Just go. Follow your heart and go.

My own life has taken an entirely new perspective since joining the Red Sox. I understand so much more about myself and my relationship with the Lord. The Lord is always teaching us, whether or not we understand how or why He is doing so.

I even have a new perspective on the Himes situation in Chicago. It's not that I see Larry in a whole new light. But had the Lord not allowed his presence to enter my life, I probably wouldn't have been able to live my dream of playing until I was forty. The day-in, day-out grind of having to play in the outfield would have proba-bly done me in much sooner. Instead, I got the chance to live my dream. The Lord has answered my prayers—and in a way that I could never have had the wisdom, foresight, or understanding to contem-plate on my own.

For this and every other blessing in my life—from my family, friends, health, and teammates, all the way down to the roof over our heads, the air we breath, and the food we eat—I have no one to thank but the Lord. Thank you, Mamma, for leading me to Him. Thank You, Lord Jesus, for never forsaking me, for always being there, for continually forgiving me, and for answering all of my prayers.

I'm waiting, listening, and ready, Lord, to take the next step, to keep on striving to do Your will. May each person reading this book and everyone everywhere feel the love You have for them. May they also see the blessings they are to each other, and may they find the faith within themselves to do Your will and thus live the full, uncompro-mised, and joyous lives that You wish for each one of us.

Amen.